TESTIMONIALS

As an expert in the field of public relations, I've helped many companies improve their public image. But one problem leaders can't afford to overlook is the image they have with their customers. Shelle's book reveals why customers get upset and what can be done about it.

—Dan Janal
President, PRLEADS.com

Your knowledge about customer cues and ability to translate that for each audience is absolutely invaluable.

—Eleanor Reynolds-Barrett
Director, Client Strategies, RBC Insurance

Shelle, the influencing tools you present, work. You use what you teach. You demonstrate how to reach rapport with people and give my group tools that help them deal with difficult people.

—Al Gonta
Director, Woodbridge Foam Corporation, St. Peters, Missouri

When it comes to customer service it's easy to find books about the effect. Shelle Rose Charvet's book is about the cause, the effect, and the solution. It's the whole picture and it will make you an expert.

—Nicholas Boothman
Author of How to Make People Like You in 90 Seconds or Less

This book tells corporate leaders how to revamp their customer service philosophies at every operational level. Rose Charvet first contrasts typical customer philosophies, and how these philosophies influence the customer experience. With short case studies, sample dialog, scripts, tables, and templates, Rose Charvet teaches readers exactly how to respond to customer emotions, stay in rapport with the customer, ask the right questions, understand customer expectations, clarify what the customer wants, make amends, and create a positive image in the customer's mind.

As an author, business consultant, corporate trainer, and business owner, Shelle Rose Charvet is the consummate expert on business communication skills. *The Customer Is Bothering Me* is an indispensible manual for customer service training.

—Dr. Judith E. Pearson
Writer, Speaker and Solution-oriented Coach

I knew as soon as I first came across Shelle's previous book, *Words That Change Minds*, that the LAB Profile would change the way I approach communicating with everyone, in both my personal and business life. Shelle's new book, *The Customer Is Bothering Me*, provides a welcome shortcut to help with one of the most critical communication challenges in business, dealing with customers. It's a perfect way to discover just how useful the LAB Profile is; it captures Shelle's experience and delivers it in a practical and pragmatic framework that anyone can use.

—Martin Hill
VP Marketing, Lawson Enterprise Software

The power of this book is that it answers the question, "Why don't they get it?" from the point of view of both customers and service/product providers. In these times, leaders are struggling for real help. We want more than simply admiring the problem or some "rah, rah" philosophy. We're all looking for something practical that we can apply tomorrow with a difficult customer. Shelle, you have done just that. This book is usable, applicable, and best of all—eminently practical. It works in the real world. I know what I'm giving my staff for Christmas.

—Jim Love, FCMC
   CEO, Chelsea Consulting Group

It's fascinating how people who deal with emotional clients on a regular basis appreciate Shelle's "upset customer process." What doesn't feel intuitive at first, truly is once you understand the motivations at play and the desired outcomes. It's win-win for your staff and your clients.

—Jan MacVinnie
   Manager, Cancer Information Service, Canadian Cancer Society

Customers, existing or potential, often cannot articulate what they truly need and want. The Customer Is Bothering Me uncovers the motivation patterns that drive customer behavior. This book is an excellent resource for anyone who can influence how customers experience your company and your products.

—Joanna Castellano
   Consumer Insights and Branding Expert
   President, Q:Quest Inc.

Here at Hewlett-Packard we talk about the total customer experience, as we want to delight our customers every day. This book is a constant reminder of just how poorly customers are being treated today and how we can obtain a competitive advantage by treating them well. I believe Shelle's book will help you understand and communicate with your customers in a whole new way—and be more successful as a result.

—Brian Campkin
   Director of Sales, Hewlett-Packard Canada

The key thing that Words That Change Minds and now The Customer Is Bothering Me have given me is the ability to plug in to the unconscious motivators of the client and to motivate them positively. My client group is not macho business folk—they are parents, most of whom want to be good parents but some of them have abused or neglected their children and caused them developmental problems. The inspiration from Shelle's work has enabled me to make a real positive difference to these children and their families—something which I am sure Shelle never intended—but which she is entitled to feel very good about.

—John Turner
   UK

Using Shelle's book I recently ran a workshop to create our customer philosophy to sell more. This provided a platform for the sales team to embark on an emotional journey from the customers' perspective and create their strategy to re-engage with customers in a powerful way. Highly motivating and inspirational. The sales team is energised to walk the talk and deliver exceptional growth!

—Gemma Norman
   Business Improvement Leader, UK

ACKNOWLEDGMENTS

I'd like to thank particularly two of my clients, Al Gonta and Brian Acker, for the pleasure of working with them and for their contributions to this book. My hat's off to Brendan McCarthy for all his work implementing a complete Customer Philosophy, Recruitment, and Management Strategy using the LAB Profile and his own knowledge and wisdom. Brendan, your case study shines a light on all the important points in this book. And thanks to David Klaasen and Dr. Pamela Campanelli for their revealing study on what prevents people from responding to surveys.

Thanks to Katherine Coy for your work editing the book. Thanks to Melody Lidstone, who makes my workday easier and more fun. And thanks to my boys, Jason and Sam Charvet and my partner, Michael Tschichholz, whose support and encouragement was much needed and appreciated. And to my Mum, Betty Rose, who is always proud of me.

Shelle Rose Charvet

Shelle Rose Charvet's

KEY CONCEPTS

WORDS THAT CHANGE MINDS: POWER PRINCIPLES

Everything you do influences the emotional state of your customer.

Everything you do determines what your customer believes about your organization.

WORDS THAT CHANGE MINDS: INFLUENCING PRINCIPLES

To get people to go somewhere with you, you need to meet them where they are and not just pretend they are already where you want them to be.

Go to their bus stop, and from their bus stop, invite them on the bus to take them where you want them to be.

BUS STOP

WORDS THAT CHANGE MINDS: PROBLEM-SOLVING PRINCIPLE

Human beings cannot be emotional and logical at the same time.

If they are upset, you need to deal with the emotions first and then the problem.

THE BAD EXPERIENCE REALITY

A bad experience as a customer can imprint a negative emotional state in the body and be recalled and relived in detail years later.

CONTENTS

PART 1

Are Your Customers Bothering You?

INTRODUCTION

How Words Change Customers' Minds

Your customers pay attention to how you attract and treat them. If you do not understand what truly motivates them, they are likely to get their needs met elsewhere. The "one size fits all" approach has become a sign of disrespect.

If you design customer processes, manage teams who communicate with customers and potential customers, or deal directly with them yourself, you are responsible for what your customers experience, and this book was written for you.

Topics in this book:

- Get your customers to buy more
- Navigate the Great Customer Attitude Shift
- Get your front line ready to handle any customer
- Avoid losing customers and staff
- The new rules for mass marketing and direct marketing
- The real reasons why organizations mismanage their customers' experience
- Why an apology is never enough
- Decode how your customers actually think and make decisions
- Deal with upset customers to create enduring loyalty
- Create a Customer Philosophy that gets and keeps customers

Demonstrating that you comprehend your customers is enormously profitable. The risk of not doing so is enormously dangerous.

Drake called his mobile phone company to discuss the charges on his bill. He was certain that he was overpaying and wanted to find out about long-distance savings plans. The call center representative told him that he was not eligible for a plan since he was already on a family calling plan. Drake became frustrated and couldn't understand why he could not have both plans, *since he calls his family and also makes many long-distance calls for his work. The rep raised her tone slightly and repeated that he could not have both: those were the rules. Incensed, Drake demanded to speak to her supervisor, who merely repeated what the rep told him. Drake threatened to move to a new provider, and the supervisor told him that it would cost him $200 for each of his four phones to get out of the contract. Drake could not believe his ears, hung up, and called three other mobile phone companies.*

In two short conversations, two representatives of the mobile phone company motivated Drake to make three phone calls to find an alternative supplier. They simply followed their normal procedure for explaining the rules. Unfortunately, their customer was not interested in the normal procedure; he had a need he wanted met. If each of the phone company staff had handled the call in a slightly different manner, they could have kept Drake's good will and probably his business.

Solving communication issues has been and will remain a constant challenge, whether in our personal lives, in the workplace with colleagues and customers, or in international relations. Technical expertise is necessary, but insufficient. You might have a state-of-the-art product, but if your customers do not feel that you (or your organization) care what happens to them, they are likely to start looking for alternative suppliers. When big financial groups encourage large numbers of consumers to acquire unsustainable mortgages or mortgages with hidden interest rate hikes and other prohibitive conditions and then foreclose, this is a failure of both communication and ethics. When partnerships fall apart and relationships fail, when projects don't succeed and enterprises go under, it is very often owing to poor communication of one kind or another.

Good communication relies essentially on being able to do the following:

- Understand what motivates individuals and groups so you can effectively get your message across
- Resolve differences in opinions and desires to some level of mutual satisfaction among the involved parties
- Inspire people to think differently or to take action

This is at the heart of what this book is about. **It is even more important during difficult business climates to excel at solving communication issues, creating positive relationships, and inspiring customers and employees to act.**

For many years I have helped my clients, positioning them to achieve the results they desire.

Why did I write *The Customer Is Bothering Me?* My first book, *Words That Change Minds: Mastering the Language of Influence*, described the many applications of the Language and Behavior Profile (LAB Profile) in understanding, predicting, and influencing behavior. **The LAB Profile[1] is a tool that enables one to understand what motivates a person or group outside of their normal awareness: essentially, at a below-conscious level.** It determines the internal thinking and decision-making processes.

Since the publication of *Words That Change Minds*, I have received and continue to receive many requests for help. Some of the requests included:

- Rewriting or creating marketing pieces and sales processes for organizations to trigger the motivation of their customers and potential customers
- Creating learning programs in high-stakes negotiation, marketing, and sales for clients in several industries
- Positioning products and services against very large competitors
- Assistance in recruiting key executive positions
- Teaching managers, team leaders, and contact center professionals to deal with upset customers and create customer loyalty
- Training front-line government employment center staff in handling upset and potentially violent clients

Other companies have asked for my assistance in solving some of their most difficult communication problems. In the auto parts industry, I helped experienced sales managers negotiate long-term multi-million-dollar contracts with the automakers. I assisted executives to keep their staff motivated after successive waves of layoffs during the period when auto sales dried up and car manufacturers received huge bailouts from government. I trained labor negotiators, one group of whom obtained the first five-year agreement in the history of their company, avoiding an expected strike.

Many organizations have been conducting below-conscious customer experience research resulting in the redesign of marketing, sales, and service strategies using this LAB Profile method. It has helped them develop answers to meet the deep unspoken needs of their customers. The LAB Profile is also extremely useful in solving conflicts and complex problems.[2]

Since 1998, I have conducted an annual LAB Profile Consultant/ Trainer Certification Program. Through this program, qualified business leaders, consultants, trainers, coaches, and marketing and human resource professionals master the skills required to use and train the LAB Profile.

---

[1] The LAB Profile was originally developed by Rodger Bailey and comes out of the field known as Neuro-Linguistic Programming (NLP). For a complete reference on the basics of this tool, please see *Words That Change Minds: Mastering the Language of Influence*.

[2] For complex problem solving, please see *Solving Communication Problems with the LAB Profile*, a one-hour CD/MP3 by Shelle Rose Charvet, available from www.WordsThatChangeMinds.com.

For people who have not participated in this sophisticated training, here is the issue: my first book introduced each of the LAB Profile Motivation Triggers and Internal Processing Patterns and gave examples from managing, marketing, sales, and recruitment as to how to use them. But, most situations are not simply a matter of one Motivation Trigger operating at a time for an individual, a small group, or even the population at large. **Often a complex *sequence* of combination patterns is at play,** and skill is needed to understand and work with this. As a result, **this book will clarify the complexity at the heart of customer-supplier interactions**. My goal is to give leaders and organizations more guidance and different strategies on how to attract and interact with their customers, resolve conflicts or issues in the sales relationship, and keep the customer happy.

The title of this book—*The Customer Is Bothering Me!*—reflects how many customers feel about how they are treated by their suppliers. This attitude has crept into Canadian customer service and made itself at home, and I believe this attitude is also present in many other places outside of Canada.

In this book, we will apply the principles of the LAB Profile methodology to the interactions between customers and suppliers in order to improve sales and your customers' experience, dramatically improving your bottom line.

This book is based on the following principles:

WORDS THAT CHANGE MINDS: CUSTOMER PRINCIPLE

Everything you do affects the emotional state of your customer.

Everything you do determines what your customer believes about your organization.

We will cover how to use language and actions to create powerfully positive emotional states in your customers and how to transform upset customers into loyal customers.

Example:

I needed to have a ring cut off my finger and wondered who could provide that service. My first thought was to go to a hardware store. I then envisioned a big guy holding a buzz saw over my finger and rapidly decided against that option. Fearfully I asked a colleague for advice. She suggested I call a certain jeweler. He came to the phone immediately, and said, "Come in anytime. We have a special machine that does it. It only takes a minute to do it."

Imagine my relief as I hung up the phone. He had reassured me; my problem was going to be easily and painlessly solved.

Ten out of ten for customer service.

Here's a different example:

I phoned my computer service company a day before leaving on a trip to find out if my kids' computer was ready (since I had not heard from them). The customer service representative demanded, "Well, when did you bring it in?" I replied that I had brought it in the previous week. "There was a huge snowstorm, you know," she continued. Trying to keep my cool, I asked if it was ready. "I don't know, I'll have to check." A few minutes later, she let me know that it wasn't finished and that the technician was out, so she didn't know when it would be ready.

Two out of ten for customer service. (Although she did take the initiative to find out that the technician wasn't there!) Can you see the angry smoke pouring from my ears? Based on this telephone conversation, I now believed:

- The company had no process to track repairs being done
- The client service representative would not take any initiative to help me with my problem
- Next time I'd better check the weather before I brought a computer in for repair!

But wait, there's more. Now, as an *angry* customer, I'm more likely to cause problems for her, because I believe that I am going to have to fight to get my computer fixed.

To the above customer principle let's add the following:

WORDS THAT CHANGE MINDS: PERSUASION PRINCIPLES

To get people to go somewhere with you, you need to meet them where they are and not just pretend they are already where you want them to be.

Go to their bus stop, and from their bus stop, invite them on the bus to take them where you want them to be.

BUS STOP

This book will help you find the emotional and psychological bus stop where your customers are waiting, and give you the language and behavior to get them on your bus.

This is an easy-to-understand principle but a difficult-to-perform behavior. When you read the solutions for upset customers, much of what I will be proposing might seem self-evident. The hard part is to actually make the correct behaviors happen. This book will help you understand, predict, and influence the customer's behavior, and for that, we need to be able to sit firmly in the customer's shoes. In my experience working with people in customer service, they are very able to remember what it is like to be a customer. However, only a few of them use this felt knowledge when they are actually marketing to, selling to, or serving customers. That's why it's both easy and difficult.

Research has shown repeatedly that solving customer problems can be highly profitable, especially when done right away and to the customer's satisfaction. When you can do this, you also avoid incurring costs to your organization. How? By preventing escalations and the negative word-of-mouth that can start so easily when customers are dissatisfied. I make presentations to many, many people each year, and I often describe the relationship I've had with my mobile phone company by saying I feel like "a prisoner" of the company. "Hello. My name is Shelle Rose Charvet and I am a prisoner of . . ."

Many organizations still use demographic studies to understand their customers. While this may help with understanding broad demographic trends, such as the current predilections of baby boomers or the values and behavior of Generation X or Y, I believe this is inadequate without understanding the deep, below-conscious motivations of the specific target audiences for your products and services. To address this need, a number of psychometric profiling tools were developed, as many marketing and branding experts became aware that demographics and past behavior analyses weren't enough to truly understand their audience.

The pressure is on. **If your company does not have a powerful way to understand and meet your customers' below-conscious needs, your competitors will soon.** The LAB Profile provides the means to more easily comprehend what customers need and to know exactly how to approach them. But it is not a simplistic tool. It does not reduce large groups of people into simple categories. It allows for the variations inherent in mass marketing, and the complex decision-making processes required when multiple purchasers are involved in large buying decisions and the servicing of customers and end users.

We will focus on these below-conscious motivations that influence customers' beliefs, as well as their behaviors in sales, service, and both business-to-consumer and business-to-business applications. I have placed particular emphasis on dealing with upset customers. It is obvious that prevention is easier than a cure, but since no one can always provide perfect products and services, having the right cure is indispensable. I will cover how to use the LAB Profile to calm upset customers and reset the course with them.

First, we will look at **Customer Philosophy and how it impacts your customers' experience**. Secondly, we will examine customer rage to **uncover the deeper meaning of explosive emotions and what to do about them**. Then we will delve into **how organizations cause their own customer experience problems**. After that, we will reveal the Words That Change Minds Customer Transaction Process and Words That Change Minds Upset Customer Process to transform how your organization and staff relate to your customers.

An insurance contact center customer service representative reported to me that a customer screamed at her because he had received incorrect advice on his insurance policy. Pushed to the wall after trying to appease the customer using several different strategies, she decided to use the Words That Change Minds Upset Customer Process. Here's what she told me:

> I raised my voice, and I said, "So this is the wrong policy!? And they told you that it would work but it didn't work out for you!? I'd better find out what happened!" At first there was a heavy silence on the other end of the line, and then the customer said in a much calmer voice, "Yes, it really does need to be checked out and I appreciate your understanding."

She investigated the problem, found a better alternative for her customer, and got back to him. That was when she got the surprise. It turned out that the gentleman on the phone was the president of a sister company in the same financial group. He told her who he was, thanked her for how she dealt with him, and sent a letter of recommendation to her boss. She had no way of knowing that this was an important customer. She had been somewhat reluctant to try out the strategy I had suggested, but when the standard approaches failed to calm her customer, she felt she had no alternative. She was surprised and pleased with the outcome. She could not have tried it out on a better client! In Chapter 7, you'll read about the four-step Words That Change Minds Upset Customer Process she used and how it applies directly to customer interactions.

Lastly, we will cover how to use the principles for designing mass communication, creating a positive customer experience, and how to ensure continual improvement at the individual, team, and organizational levels.

I'll discuss them in Part 5. We will also cover advanced applications of the LAB Profile for use in:

- Handling problem interactions between customers and suppliers
- Hiring and recruitment
- Systems implications such as creating your Trigger of Change Mechanisms

In Appendix A, I've summarized the main concepts and suggested exercises for team leaders that can be used with front-line teams. The other appendices contain useful shortcuts and resources to help you use the LAB Profile in many other ways.

It is my hope that you will find useful ideas here, whether you create the systems that will ultimately serve your customers, directly lead teams that serve customers, or serve customers yourself. Some of these ideas will seem to be common sense, while others are based on uncommon sense—decoding motivations that are typically outside most people's awareness.

The only way to know if any of this works is to test it out for yourself. Please let me know what you think.

Shelle Rose Charvet
shelle@WordsThatChangeMinds.com

CHAPTER 1

Which Words Change Customers' Minds: The LAB Profile Patterns

Increasingly, as customers have become more and more difficult to deal with, suppliers have needed better ways of understanding them. We needed a mechanism for tracking what truly motivates customers and how their motivation shifts from time to time and place to place. The LAB Profile is a subtle psycho-linguistic tool (that is, it's based on the words people use) that enables us to understand motivation and thinking patterns, whether it be for mass marketing or one-to-one communication. **With relatively small verbal shifts, one can influence major communication problems or find the open door in what appears to be a closed mind.**

C AA

CASE STUDY

For the Canadian Automobile Association (CAA), I taught their marketing department to understand people's primary motivation for becoming members of the CAA and therefore how to market and sell services to them. Their problem was to get new members to renew after their first year of membership. Their research told them that if a new member had not used any of the other benefits that come from membership in the first year, they were much less likely to renew.

Research had also shown that CAA members' primary motivation for becoming members was to *avoid* having a problem on the road when traveling by car. They were not initially motivated by other benefits that could be gained from membership. Therefore the language used to communicate with members needed to be what we call "Away From" Language—that is, wording that describes problems which can be prevented or solved by membership—rather than "Toward" Language, which would outline the benefits gained through membership.

The CAA sales staff learned how to sell other benefits to members by using the same Away From Language. Instead of promoting their free TripTiks simply as route maps, they began to talk about how they could help clients "avoid getting lost." They could book your hotel, so you "wouldn't have to worry about where to stay" on your route. This switch in language helped them increase the use of these services, and ensured that many more members renewed their memberships.

A friend of mine wanted to motivate her brother to go on vacation for a week with her. Once she realized her brother was much more Reactive than she was, she stopped using Proactive Language such as "Let's go! Let's just go, come on, let's just do it!" which incites a person immediately into action, and she began to say things that matched how her brother actually got motivated. When she said to him, "I'd like you to think about whether or not you'd like to go away on holiday with me to such and such a place, because I suspect it might be something you would like. Please let me know what you think," this Reactive Language invited her brother to do what he preferred to do: to reflect on the idea and consider it. He thought about her offer this time, and accepted immediately.

Knowing someone's LAB Profile Patterns will help you prevent and solve communication problems.[1] You can decode the factors that motivate people as they are making a purchase or speaking with customer service. These motivations can and do shift when customers are having different experiences, which means organizations need to know how to anticipate the patterns and respond to the shifts as they occur in order to meet their customers' varying needs. I'll show you how to do just that in the sections that follow.

The Shift between Normal and Problem Transactions

In this book, I have described strategies for handling the huge shifts in customer motivation that plague many organizations. While we are all aware that customer behavior and motivation are different during a normal transaction versus during a problem transaction, many organizations are very poor at identifying and responding to this shift. Normal transactions tend to be routine—what we call Procedural in LAB Profile terms, when the customer is concentrating on a task or some *thing* they need to do or get (a Thing Pattern in LAB Profile terms).

However, when a customer has an issue or problem, he is no longer willing to follow the supplier's normal procedure. He is much more likely

---

[1] See Appendix B for a complete LAB Profile Questionnaire.

to want to *find a way around the normal procedure* in order to get the problem solved and is willing to break any rules necessary to do so. This is one reason that upset customers are so difficult to deal with—they do not want to do what you tell them to do. Using the LAB Profile to decode the Motivation Patterns behind this kind of shift, you can meet your customer's deepest unspoken needs.

There are two kinds of LAB Profile Patterns:

1. **The Motivation Triggers:** these describe how people get motivated and *why* they need to be interested in something.
2. **The Working Traits:** these describe internal mental processes and how a person becomes convinced of something.

Here's how it works: You decode what is driving a person or group by analyzing the language structure that they use. You can determine this by interviewing a representative group of prospects or actual customers. You can also watch their behavior to identify the Patterns at play. This is easier than it looks at first, and there are guidelines in this book to show you exactly how to do this. In this chapter, you will learn what the Patterns are and how to identify them.

After you have identified their LAB Profile Patterns, the next step is to use the appropriate Influencing Language in order to **influence how the customer thinks and gets motivated. This is how you can dramatically increase your impact and response rate.** The LAB Profile is now used to research and create marketing materials and to design sales processes based on what we know will motivate prospective customers.[2]

The Influencing Language associated with each Pattern, illustrated later in this chapter, enables you to match the precise sequences and ways that people get motivated and process information. Using the right Influencing Language will enable you to dramatically increase your impact, make more sales, change perceptions, and reduce resistance. It is the same idea as having two people speak the same language, as opposed to trying to communicate by having one person speak Chinese and the other Arabic.

LAB Profile Pattern Descriptions

The Motivation Triggers and Working Traits outlined here in the LAB Profile Patterns describe a person's preferences in a given situation. This is about motivation and behavior, and is *not* a personality profile: **as people's be-**

---

[2] I do this kind of work for my clients, as do many of the Certified LAB Profile Consultant/Trainers.

havior and motivation changes from Context to Context, so will their LAB Profile Patterns. A person's LAB Profile Patterns are very likely to be different when they are buying toilet paper as opposed to when they are on vacation. Please refer to Appendices B and C for the LAB Profile Questionnaire and Influencing Language Short Cuts.

How exactly does a person trigger and maintain their interest level in a given situation? Conversely, what will de-motivate them? For example, if a person prefers to take the initiative in her work but finds herself having to wait a long time, she will soon become frustrated and de-motivated. Similarly, if customers are motivated to get something *now*, but they are made to wait, they are likely to become angry. If you can quickly identify what your customer needs and adapt to that, you are much more likely to keep the happy customer or regain a happy customer by resolving their issues in the particular way that suits them.

Below is a description of each of the LAB Profile Categories and Patterns for the Motivation Triggers and the Working Traits and the Influencing Language to use with each one. These Patterns will help you use the four-step Words That Change Minds Customer Transaction Process and the Words That Change Minds Upset Customer Process in Chapters 6 and 7.

Motivation Triggers

1. Level Category

Does the person prefer to take the initiative (Proactive) or wait, think, and consider (Reactive)? Many people are right in the middle with this category and so seem to be neither very Proactive nor very Reactive. It is really only important to notice if your customer seems to be very Proactive (they want what they want right now!!) or very Reactive (it is difficult to extract a decision from them). The typical definitions of Proactive and Reactive in the business environment are not quite the same as the following definitions of the Proactive and Reactive Patterns from the LAB Profile.

Proactive

These people are motivated by doing and initiating. At the extreme they will act with little or no thinking. They want things done now and hate to wait. As customers, they can be impatient and may seem hard to handle or aggressive. If you can give them what they want right away, they will jump at the opportunity and not hesitate to buy. If you can't, they will go buy somewhere else right away.

Proactive customers respond best when you use the following phrases: **let's do it now; I'll get on it right away; let's not wait for this; I'll make it happen; let's just go for it; I'll do it right now; no need to sit around waiting.**

Reactive

When customers are in Reactive mode, they prefer to wait, analyze, consider, and think. During difficult times, they may wait endlessly and have difficulty making a decision. To get these customers to say yes, you will need to let them think it through thoroughly and have them think about the problems caused by waiting any longer (see also Away From) and the advantages of getting started as soon as possible (see also Toward).

Reactive customers respond best when the following phrases are used: **when you think this through; it's best to understand what will happen; let's think about it; after having analyzed; having thoroughly understood the issues; what do you think now?** The key is to enable them to complete the thinking process so that a decision can be made. (Notice that I said "a decision can be made" rather than "make a decision." Using the passive voice is a good match for Reactive customers.)

2. Criteria

Criteria are the words, phrases, and images that customers use to indicate that something has a particular importance for them. Criteria can be positive or negative. They are a person's labels for their values in a given Context. Because these phrases and images have a special importance, when a customer sees or hears their Criteria, they will have a positive emotional and physical reaction.

It is a critical part of the sales and service process to find out what is important to your client. When I was looking for a new car, I visited seven dealerships. Only one salesperson in seven asked me what I wanted and what was important to me in a new car. I did mention to another salesperson that he had not asked me what was important to me, and he replied that during the conversation we had been having, he had been able to figure it out. "Oh, good," I replied, "then what *is* important to me about a new car?" He was unable to tell me.

To discover your customers' Criteria, you can ask them:

> **What do you want?**
> **What is important to you about . . . ?**
> **What does it have to have, or what does it have to do for you?**

Note your customer's answers to these questions word for word and **build them into your suggestions and proposals, since these phrases are key motivators for your customer.**

3. Direction Category

What Direction is the customer moving in? Are they heading Toward something they want or trying to Move Away from a problem or negative consequence of some kind? When you know the Direction, you can match your language and processes to exactly the right motivator. For example, if your customer needs to fix a flat tire, they want to get rid of that problem (i.e., move *Away From* the problem). Your choice of words should reflect this direction; talk about removing the flat, getting rid of the broken tire, or patching up the tire so the problem will not occur again, rather than using Toward Language such as "getting you back on the road" or "making sure everything is working."

Toward

These customers want to achieve a goal or are motivated to gain a benefit. They tend to be focused on what they want. For them to make a decision or take action, they will need a goal or benefit to move toward. They will buy a carrot, not a stick.

Customers with a Toward Trigger respond best when the following words or phrases are used: **here is what you want; the benefits of this are; when you do this the positive consequences are; here is what you will attain, obtain, have, get, achieve; the goal here is to.**

Away From

These people are motivated to avoid what they do not want and to solve problems. These customers will jump into action to prevent certain things from happening. Credible threats will make them move away. They are more likely to purchase or agree in order to prevent a consequence or solve an issue rather than gain a benefit. For example, they may buy something now to avoid having to spend more money later. Or they may be preoccupied with what is wrong with your proposal.

People with an Away From Trigger respond best when the following words and phrases are used: **here's how you can avoid this problem; if it's not solved now it will only get worse; do you see any problems with this proposal?; why not fix it now so it won't deteriorate; avoid this; never have to deal with this again; prevent these negative consequences; if you don't now; steer clear of; get rid of; solve; fix.**

The Question to Determine Direction

Why is that [Criterion] important?

If the customer tells you what they want, they are in Toward mode. If they talk about what they do not want, they are in Away From mode. You can ask the question more than once to find out the why of the why, the problem of the problem (Away From), or the goal of the goal (Toward).

4. Source Category

Is the customer more motivated by external influences or by judging for themselves using their own internal standards? Sometimes people are influenced to make a decision by others they respect, or by facts and figures, and sometimes they prefer to decide for themselves. When you know the Source of your customer's decision-making, you can tailor your persuasion strategy to give them the right information or to take them on a journey where they can discover things for themselves.

Internal

These customers are motivated to decide based on their own internal standards and Criteria. They do not want to be told what to do. Bold statements and Command Language[3] will raise their resistance. If you have firmly established your credibility with your prospective customers, you can be directive from time to time, but it is still best to invite Internal customers to decide for themselves.

Customers who are in an Internal mode respond best to the following words and phrases and generally to the **Language of Suggestion:[4] only you can decide; does this meet your criteria?; what do you think?; here's some information you may want to consider; may I make a suggestion?**

External

Customers who are in External mode are influenced by outside information or other people. They may need reassurance from someone they respect before they will buy. When Wayne Gretzky encourages people to buy

---

[3] Command Language is the imperative or any verbal form where you are telling someone what to do: "Sign up now"; "Apply right away"; "You've got to see this." Many calls to action overuse Command Language and turn off Internal people.

[4] The Language of Suggestion is an invitation for people to take the invitation and judge for themselves. See examples above. This is the preferred way to persuade customers with an Internal Motivation Trigger.

a Ford, or when Sarah Jessica Parker uses a particular Garnier brand hair color, the idea is to persuade External shoppers to follow their example.

Customers with an External Motivation Trigger respond best to the following words and phrases: **this is a list of our customers; here's what people are saying about this; so and so thinks; the feedback you'll get; I'd appreciate it if you would; the approval you'll get; others will notice; studies prove; you should** (Command Language—use only when you have impeccable credibility).

Questions to Determine Source

How do you know you have done a good job at . . .?
(e.g., purchasing a software package for your company)

How would you know if you had done a good job at . . .?
(e.g., buying a car for you and your family)

If the customer indicates that she knows and describes how she decided for herself, she is operating from an Internal Pattern. If she does not know, or if she indicates an outside influence, she is more External.

5. Reason Category

Does a customer prefer having choices and alternatives, or are they more interested in following a step-by-step process in making a decision or using a product or service? This category describes differences in how customers reason through a buying decision; either they want lots of choices (and may have trouble picking only one option) or they want a straightforward method and are motivated to complete the process. The words you use with these two types of customers can either dramatically increase your business or risk turning people off at key moments, so it is critical to notice which mode your customers are in.

Options

They are motivated to go outside the normal process, to bend or break rules, and want to have options and choices. It can be harder to get them to commit because that would entail eliminating some options in order to choose only one. They like to think outside the box and are prepared to go around the procedure to get what they want. If prospective customers stay in an Options mode, it means they are still considering alternatives and they are not yet ready to buy.

People in Options mode respond best when the following words and phrases are used: **normally we are supposed to . . . but let's . . . ; this time we'll break the rules; opportunity; choices; here are the options; there are other alternatives; either/or; here's what else might be useful; this is one way to do it; let's look at the possibilities.**

Procedures

These customers prefer a step-by-step process and like to complete what they start. They are interested in how to do something: how to buy, how to use, how to fix. When they have a question, they want a clear step-by-step method as the answer, without alternatives. They believe there is a right way to do things. If you give them too many choices when they do not have a procedure for deciding, they may not make up their minds. When customers switch to Procedures Language, it means they are ready to commit.

Customers in Procedures mode respond best when the following approach is used: **speak the steps (i.e., first . . . then . . . after which . . . next . . . lastly); tell them how it works; how to buy; the right way; tried and true; the way; the method; the process; step-by-step.** Make sure you let them know where the last step is because they are motivated to complete the process.

Questions to Discover Reason

Why did you choose . . . ? (e.g., your last music system)
Why would you choose . . . ? (e.g., a particular enterprise software system)

If your customer tells you a story about *how* they got their last music system, they are in Procedures mode. If they give you a *list of reasons why* they chose, they are in Options mode.

6. Decision Factors Category

How does a person react to change and what frequency of change do they need? Are your customers constantly looking for something brand new? Do they want products and services that are mainly the same with some improvements (an evolution), or would they prefer the products and services to stay the same as before? What kind of relationship do they want with you? One they can always count on, one that evolves, or one that is constantly in flux? It is important to determine these client desires to avoid turning them off.

Sameness

These customers want to be able to count on what they usually get. They are attracted to what is familiar. Many customers, for example, want to deal with the same person from their suppliers and need that feeling of familiarity. Software end-users with a Sameness Pattern typically hate it when their favorite packages change their look or the instructions for how to use them change.

Customers in Sameness mode respond best when the following words or phrases are used: **this is the same as; what this has in common with the previous edition; you use this just the same as you always have; like before; unchanged; as you know already; classic; as we've always done.**

Sameness with Exception

These customers prefer gradual improvement and evolution in the products and services they use. They are motivated when they believe something is better than before. They will be interested in enhancements and improvements to what they are already using.

Customers in Sameness with Exception mode respond best when the following words or phrases are used: **this is more than before; it's better; there is less hassle with this; fewer errors; it's the same except; evolving; there is a progression in how it works; gradual improvement; upgrade; honed.**

Difference

These clients are your early adopters. They are attracted to what is new and different in your products and services. Sometimes they believe it is they themselves who are different. I have had prospective clients ask me if I have worked in their particular kind of business before, because it is a "different kind of business," or sometimes they have told me that their business is "very different" from others in the sector.

Customers with a Difference Pattern respond best when the following words or phrases are used: **this is a new process; it is totally different from what is on the market; this year's model is completely changed; switch; shift; unique; revolutionary; brand new.**

Sameness with Exception and Difference

These are clients who are attracted to both evolutionary and revolutionary change. Your products need to be both new and improved. They may reveal their Pattern by asking you how something is "different or better."

People with this Motivation Trigger respond best when both Sameness with Exception and Difference phrases are used. For example: **new and better; a totally different approach with improvements; completely changed; progressively new; upgrade with changes; brand new with more; different because it's honed.**

Questions to Uncover Decision Factors

What is the relationship between [your present home] *and the last one?*

What is the relationship between [the way you presently process invoices] *and the way you did it before?*

If they tell you what is *the same, not changed*, this is the Sameness Pattern. If they talk about how they are *similar, but more of this, less of that*, then it is Sameness with Exception. If they *do not understand the question or only notice what is different or new*, this is a Difference Pattern. If they talk about what is *similar and different or new*, this is Sameness with Exception and Difference.

Working Traits

The Working Traits explain how people go about processing information, what they pay attention to, and how they go about becoming convinced. These categories describe the internal processing habits rather than what will trigger a customer's motivation. Remember, as with the Motivation Triggers, Working Traits may change based on the Context or situation that the person is in. For example, some customers prefer to know all the details when they are purchasing a new high-tech camera, but then just want an overview of features and benefits for the purchase of a dishwasher. Similarly, I may be very Thing-oriented when I am conducting a normal transaction at a financial institution, but want to speak to a person when thinking about investing.

1. Scope Category

How much information does a customer need in a given situation? Do they prefer just the general overview, all the detailed information, or somewhere in between? When dealing with large groups of customers, it is better to give an overview and then the option for getting more details, in order to accommodate both preferences without making people wade through information that does not interest them.

Specific

Specific customers pay attention to only their specific area of interest, and they want all the information available about it. They like details. Sometimes they will give you a lot of information, and therefore, they can take longer to handle on customer service calls. They tend not to see the overview and may not like it if you provide too short a summary of their needs.

Specific customers respond best when you use the following words or phrases: **exactly; here are the precise steps that we can follow; can I give you all of the specifics?; precisely; specifically** (and give lots of details).

General

These customers just want the overview, the big picture. They can handle some details for short periods of time if they are particularly interested in something. Many people have a General Pattern when they are scanning websites and will only read detailed text if something is very attractive to them. These customers may not think to give you all the information you need. Recently I had an e-mail from a prospective client who said, "We are still interested in a presentation, how can we arrange that?" and I knew that when we spoke we were going to probably be very brief. (She was also very Proactive, so we made an agreement quite quickly!)

Clients with a General Pattern respond best when the following words or phrases are used: **the big picture; essentially; the important thing is; in general; concepts; basically.** Keep your information short and to the point.

2. Attention Direction Category

Does the person pay attention to the nonverbal behavior of others and display nonverbal behavior, or does the person focus on content alone?

Self

When someone is in Self mode, they do not notice others' behavior or voice tone. They tend not to have a wide range of expressions or tone changes, and they do not give nonverbal cues. This Pattern is relatively rare. It is estimated that about seven percent of the population in the Context of work has a Self Pattern.[5]

Customers with this Pattern respond best when you **keep your communication focused on the content, and use mainly Internal Influencing Language.** This works because they pay very little attention to the level of rapport you have with them and focus mainly on the content of what you are saying. It is best to use the Internal Language of Suggestion so they do not feel you are bossing them around.

Other

Most customers will notice and respond to nonverbal behavior and also show expression and make changes in their tone of voice. Rapport is important to customers with this Pattern, and they will need to feel that you are on the same wavelength as them. **Mirror and match their body language and voice tone to establish rapport, and make sure they know that you have picked up what is important to them by playing back their Criteria.**

3. Stress Response Category

This category describes how people respond to stressful situations. For customers, not getting what they want often constitutes a very stressful situation. It is important to pay attention to your customers' emotional state when they have a problem with your products or services, since you will need to find a way (see the Words That Change Minds Upset Customer Process, Chapter 7) to deal with their emotions before you can solve their problem. Otherwise they may not cooperate with you to find a solution.

Feelings

These customers freak out when something is stressful. They tend to jump into a negative emotional state and have some difficulty calming down. They are prone to outbursts, raising their tone, and being rude. Even if you succeed at calming them down, you will need to be very careful not to set them off again.

Customers in Feelings mode need to know that you *get* the problem from their point of view. If they are upset, you need to demonstrate that

---

[5] Rodger Bailey determined the original percentages for the distribution of LAB Profile Patterns in the Context of work. While his work was not a scientific study, nor indicative of the distribution inside any particular organization or for other Contexts, it has proven over the years to be useful for estimating the likelihood of different Patterns to be present.

you are upset too—not with them, but with the problem. The Upset Customer Process in Part 4 demonstrates how to do this.

Choice

These customers may move in and out of an emotional state when the interaction does not go their way. While they may become upset, they have an easier time calming down and listening to your suggestions. They want some empathy and a solution, and are therefore willing to look at how the problem could be solved without too much upset.

They respond best when you demonstrate empathy for their situation and use phrases such as the following: **this solution feels right and makes sense in this situation** (notice both emotional and logical words); **find the answer to this that feels right; find the way to make the best of this.**

Thinking

These customers do not tend to go into a negative emotional state when they do not get what they want. They stay very logical and are probably immediately ready to look for a solution. They are unlikely to show empathy to the customer service representative, as they are not paying attention to emotions, just logic.

Customers in the Thinking Pattern respond best when the following words or phrases are used: **clear thinking; logical; rational; cold reality; hard facts and statistics.**

How to Discover Stress Response

When something goes wrong for your customer, notice how upset they get and whether or not they calm down easily. For best results when dealing with Feelings customers, use the Upset Customer Process in Part 4 and the Customer Tone Chart in Chapter 8.

4. Style Category

What kind of human working environment allows a person to be most productive and effective? This is a very useful category when hiring employees who will deal with customers. When you have people who work well around others, it is easier to train them in the customer service or sales behaviors that are best in your environment. If staff are more productive on their own, you might consider setting them up in a "back office" kind of environment. Please see the Irish Continental Case Study in Chapter 13 for a working example of how to hire for excellent customer service and sales.

Independent

When an employee is in this mode, they prefer to work by themselves with sole responsibility for the projects they are working on. When they are interrupted, they may lose their train of thought and become annoyed. They like to block out noises and other distractions from the environment so they can concentrate on their work. They are more suited to working on their own rather than with clients for long periods of time. As customers, they prefer to make decisions when on their own, without noisy distractions from salespeople or colleagues.

People in Independent Mode respond best when the following words or phrases are used: **do it alone; you can be by yourself to think about this; you alone; without interruption; you will have control of this part.**

Proximity

People in the Proximity mode like to be in control of their own work with others around in clearly defined roles. They will need to know specifically what their tasks are and will want to work in conjunction with other people (and customers), provided their roles and responsibilities are clear. This is one of the Patterns suitable for employees in call centers, sales roles, and in-person customer service. As customers, they want to know who will do what in the transaction.

Proximity people respond best when the following words or phrases are used: **you'll be in charge of . . . ; around others; you'll direct; your responsibility is [x]; theirs is [y]; you and I will each do the following.**

Cooperative

These employees prefer to work all together with others in a team, sharing responsibility. They naturally get into rapport with customers as they are "with" in spirit. To be productive and creative, they will need to be with people building ideas together, and they may tend not to get work done when they are left to their own devices. If the job requires being with customers all day long, they will enjoy the conversations and may need to be reminded of what they are there to do. As customers, they will want to work with their suppliers and will tend to take up a lot of salespeople's time as they make a decision.

People in Cooperative mode respond best when the following words or phrases are used: **us; we; together; all of us; team; group; share responsibility; do it together; let's; we can do this all together.**

5. Organization Category

Does a person pay attention to people, relationships, thoughts, and feelings, or to tasks, ideas, systems, and tools? This is an important LAB Profile Category to pay attention to, both when hiring employees to work with customers and when helping your customers. Thing employees may not be as adept at establishing rapport, since they focus on the tools or activities of the work rather than the person. (Imagine having an employee who had the following combination: Internal [decides for himself], Procedures [follows a step-by-step process], Self [does not notice nonverbals], and Thing [focuses on things]—you might have difficulty directing this employee's attention onto anything other than the things he believes are important.) Customers tend to become very Person-focused when they want to find someone to fix their problem.

Person

Employees in this mode focus on people and relationships, feelings, and thoughts. They like people and want to have good relationships. As salespeople, sometimes they can forget the job is to make a sale or complete a service procedure because they are busy communicating with the customer. These people are great at helping clients in difficulty or under stress, such as clients assisting family members in the health care system. Empathy comes naturally to Person employees. As customers, they are interested in the salespeople and want a relationship with them, and this is an important part of the decision to buy.

People in a Person mode respond when you use people's names. They also like to hear the following: **feelings; thoughts; feel good; people; relationships; this will improve your relationship; you will feel that it's right; imagine the excitement.**

Thing

Employees in this mode focus on tasks, systems, ideas, tools, things, and getting the job done. They do well serving customers when the communication is purely transactional: for example, transferring money to other accounts, giving information in answer to a technical question, etc. They tend not to be as adept at showing empathy for clients; they would rather just solve the problem. As customers, they are very focused on *what* they are buying, and not so much on the relationship.

People in Thing mode respond best when the following words or phrases are used: **things; systems; process; task; job; goal; organization; the thing to do here is**.

6. Rule Structure Category

Does a person have rules for themselves and others? This category takes a look at whether employees or customers are likely to clearly state their expectations of others, if they know what they need (or not), if they are likely to do what they want without much thought about others, or if they are able to understand that there is more than one side to a story.

My/My My Rules for Me. My Rules for You.

They know what is good for them and for other people. People with this Pattern are likely to tell others what they need or expect. These are customers who have no trouble telling you what they want and may sound very certain even when they know little about the matter at hand. Customer service employees with this pattern may become too directive with clients and may need to soften their approach.

People with this Pattern respond best when the following words or phrases are used: **you know what you want; when it's clear to you; what goes for the goose goes for the gander; the fruit doesn't fall far from the tree**.

My/. My Rules for Me. I Don't Care about You.

These are the people who know what they want and do not take into consideration what others need in the situation. Very angry customers may do this by bulldozing your customer service staff and by not recognizing their needs or the needs of your organization.

People with this Pattern respond best when you use the Language of Influence for Internal people: **only you can decide; here's a suggestion; this may be in your best interests.**

No/My Don't Know What the Rules Are for Me. My Rules for You.

These people are in a place where they are not sure what they need or how to get out of a problem. They can more easily guide others than themselves. As clients, they clearly need someone to guide them to a solution for their need. As employees, they will need instructions about what to do and how to handle exceptions to the general rules.

People in No/My mode respond best when the following words or phrases are used: **even if you aren't sure; this is what to do; here is how to handle that; what would someone else do in this situation?**

My/Your My Rules for Me. Your Rules for You.

These people know there is more than one perspective. They know that what may work for one person may be inappropriate for another. They can make good interpreters and mediators when there is a problem between a customer and another staff member. Sometimes they are hesitant to tell others what to do because they believe "different strokes for different folks, so it's not for me to tell others, as it might not work for them."

People with a My/Your Pattern respond best when the following words or phrases are used: **different strokes for different folks; not everyone is the same; each to his own; you will need to work out what is best for each party.**

7. Convincer Channel Category

When customers are going through the process of becoming convinced to buy something or make a decision, there are generally a couple of phases to this process. First they need to gather some information to inform their decision. Convincer Channel describes the type of information they need in a situation to start the process of getting convinced about something. Many people will need more than one of the Patterns below.

See

People in See mode create images in their heads to understand and process information. As customers, they need to see evidence in the information-gathering phase. If they cannot visualize what you are proposing or see it in reality, they will not fully understand your offer.

Customers who need to See respond best when the following words or phrases are used: **look; clear idea; show you; create a picture; watch; bring into focus; the writing is on the wall.** You can use **visual metaphors and literally show them** the product or service in action; hold it up for them to see.

Hear

These employees and customers like to discuss and talk over things in order to get the information they need. They respond well to oral presentations and like to hear what others say about something.

People in this mode respond best when the following words or phrases are used: **dialogue; tell; hear; talk about; gossip; rumor; word has it.**

Read

Some customers need to read about a product or service to get the required information to make a decision. Often in complex buying decisions such as the purchase of enterprise software systems, a lot of reading is required as part of the decision-making process. However, in customer service situations where the customer is upset about something, it is very rare that they will be willing to read policy when requested to do so.

People in this mode respond best when you give them a report to read. You can invite them to: **skim this paper; look in the documentation; the text explains it; it's in the e-mail; you can read all about it; can I send you some documentation to read.**

Do

These customers want to try something out to see if it fits their needs. A hands-on approach works well so they become familiar with your product or service. Clothing and cars are usually sold this way, but many services can also have a demonstration so that the prospective customer can work with the process or information.

People who need to Do respond best when the following words or phrases are used: **try this on for size; get a grasp; hang on to this idea; let's work with it; here's how to get a handle on this; try this out to feel for yourself how it works; notice how easy it is to use.**

8. Convincer Mode Category

The second phase in becoming convinced has to do with what has to happen to the information or evidence previously gathered to make a person become "convinced" of something. Each person has their own way of knowing how much information is enough.

Number of Examples

They need to have the data a certain number of times to be convinced. Slightly more than half of the population needs the data three times to be convinced about something. "Once is an incident, twice is a coincidence, and three times is a pattern." If the goal is to get a potential customer to feel comfortable or familiar with your product or service, have them experience (see, hear, read, do) it a minimum of three times. This is a great way to overcome the strangeness of a new idea or different approach if your customer is more comfortable with things they know well.

People who need information a Number of Times respond well when you say: **three** (or match their number if different than three) **times is a winner; try it out a couple of times; here are some examples of this in action; would you like another example?**

Automatic

Customers with this Convincer Mode take a small amount of information and get convinced immediately based on what they imagine. These are the folks who make snap judgments about things and then rarely change their minds. If someone dismisses you right away without gathering much information, chances are that they are in this mode.

People in Automatic mode respond best when you use words and phrases such as: **you'll know right away; it's obvious immediately what the benefits are; it's a no-brainer; you can see at once that this will fix that problem.**

Consistent

I call this Pattern the Scarlett O'Hara pattern. "Tomorrow is another day." For these people, tomorrow is a completely new day, and just because they were convinced about something one day does not mean that they will stay convinced. They are never completely convinced once and for all. I had a marketing client who was part of a group that was learning and implementing LAB Profile language into their projects. At the beginning of each monthly session, "Tessie" would come into the meeting room, plunk herself down in a chair, sigh loudly, moan about all the urgent things that needed to be done, and generally show her disapproval about wasting her time on this. By the end of each day, she would be enthusiastically contributing to the activities, but she would show up the next time with a black cloud over her head again. Every time, she needed to be re-convinced of the benefits of what we were doing.

Consistent customers need you to reestablish credibility and rapport each time you communicate with them. If you do this, you will be the rare supplier who knows how to work with them. Every time you communicate with a Consistent customer, make sure you mention their Criteria and how you are meeting their needs. Phrases to use include the following: **each time you do this you will find; test it out every time you use it; it passes the test each time; you never can be too careful.**

Period of Time

Some people do not need a specific number of times; they need to gather information for a certain duration before they are convinced. These customers may want to think it over "for a while" or mention how long they took the last time they made this kind of decision.

These people respond best to the following kinds of phrases: **how long would you like to think about this; it may take a while to know; we can look at this over the next two weeks; how long would you like to use it before you decide?**

***

In *The Customer Is Bothering Me*, the LAB Profile is used to decode and speak to the specific motivations behind normal and problem customer transactions, whether for sales or after-sales customer service. The LAB Profile will help you develop solutions to customer problems, by using the Customer Transaction Process in Chapter 6 and the Upset Customer Process in Part 4.

You can also use the LAB Profile for **designing customer communications in direct mail, marketing materials, and even advertising campaigns**. (See Chapter 12 for more information.) There are huge hiring advantages when you use the LAB Profile to design a customer-centered position. When you **use the Influencing Language to attract the candidates with the right patterns, it will make hiring and training people much easier,** since your new staff will already have the right inclinations. They will be a natural match to the LAB Profile Patterns that your customers need. Recruitment applications are explained and illustrated with an extraordinary case study in Chapter 13.

Customer motivations can be complex and varied. The LAB Profile enables you to more closely tune your language, processes, and visuals to meet your customers' needs more effectively by matching how your customers get motivated at different times in sales and service transactions. This book will also show you how to prevent and solve contentious interactions with your clients. **Call center leaders will learn how employees can solve "customer rage" before it gets out of control.**

Whether you want to improve your customers' experience, repair older processes, or design a new customer service system, this book will provide you with:

1. **A clear methodology** for determining single and complex Motivation Patterns in individuals and groups to enable you, without fail, to go to the bus stop where your customers are waiting.
2. **Influencing Language** that ensures you can get your customers on the bus!

Without an understanding of what motivates your customers and employees, communicating effectively so that you meet their needs and getting customers to buy what you have to sell, use your products and services, and derive great benefit from them is difficult at the best of times. **When the sales environment becomes more difficult, it is even more important to understand what is motivating your customers.**

Reading this book may be your first step to transforming communication and your results with your customers.

PART 2

Responding to the Great Customer Attitude Shift

CHAPTER 2

Unveiling Your Organization's Beliefs about Customers

Flying on Air Canada back to Toronto early one Sunday morning from Québec City, after delivering a two-day seminar, I was sound asleep in my chair. Suddenly a searing hot feeling flashed down my leg. Instantly awake, I jerked my head up to look at the flight attendant standing nearby, holding an urn. "You just spilled coffee down my leg!" I squawked. "It was tea," she replied.

Am I bothering your people? As hard to believe as this example is, I am certain that I am not the only customer who encounters this sort of attitude during the day-to-day activities of going to work and living life. Since I've begun collecting customer experience stories, both good and bad, they seem to be everywhere. Everywhere I go, people tell me more stories—the service they receive or don't receive really makes a mark on them, and I'm not talking just coffee or tea here!

After years of noticing the peculiarities exhibited by people serving customers, I began to wonder what was behind the weird behavior. **What are the below-conscious processes, those that operate out of people's awareness, driving their behaviors? Perhaps they are acting based on a whole philosophy they hadn't realized was there.** I decided to explore this.

Customer Philosophies in Different Countries

The Oxford Dictionary defines the word *philosophy* as a "set of beliefs." I wanted to find out what these were as they related to customer service.

The French Customer Philosophy

I lived in Paris for five years and then spent two years on a farm in Normandy while I conducted communication workshops around France and other European countries. Since then, I have visited and worked in France often and have had many opportunities to experience French customer service firsthand.

If you have been to France, this may sound familiar. My experiences have ranged from the woman behind the counter at the SNCF (the national railway) screaming at me when all I wanted to do was buy a ticket to having a car insurance agent physically throw me out of his office for saying his prices were too high. When I first moved to France, I even had difficulty getting served in restaurants. Like many Canadians, I would gingerly raise my hand to get service and whisper, *"Excusez-moi?"* This strategy guarantees that you will go to bed hungry. I was eventually tipped off by a friend that one needs to fling one's arm in the air and yell, *"S'IL VOUS PLAÎT!"* It is the only way to attract sufficient attention to get service.

Making purchases in Paris department stores can be a nightmare. First you have to find a clerk who will agree to let you buy your item. This is not easy. She might ring it up for you, take the item from you, and give you a sheet of paper with the item number and price marked on it. Next you have to line up at the cashier's desk to pay. Then you have to return to the first lady (if you can find her) to show your receipt to pick up your merchandise. And heaven help you if you display even a hint of impatience. Once a clerk shouted at me about how unreasonable I was for suggesting that it would be great if she could both take payment *and* wrap up my merchandise.

In a large upscale Paris department store, I had to ask three different sales clerks if I could purchase a couple of blouses; each one declared that she didn't handle that brand!

As this kind of occurrence seemed to be the norm, I began to hypothesize about the beliefs and values driving these behaviors. If there were a philosophy operating that made these actions understandable, what might it be? What must these people believe in order to behave that way?

One day it struck me. The French customer philosophy is:

"The customer is always wrong!"

If you really want something, you have to raise your voice and make a scene. Whatever your strategy may be to obtain good service, it's clear that, as a customer, you are always wrong.

The Canadian Customer Philosophy

When I returned home to Canada, my first impression was that sales and customer service people were *nice*. I mean *really* nice, especially considering where I was coming from. It took me quite a while to get a sense of how things really worked in Canada. The first time I went to buy groceries, I put a credit card on the counter to pay for the food. The woman behind the counter looked at me askance and said, "You're not from here?" I replied, "What do you mean?" She said, "Well, you can't buy groceries with a credit card." Having just returned from France, I yelled, "WHAT DO YOU MEAN YOU CAN'T BUY GROCERIES WITH A CREDIT CARD? YOU CAN PAY FOR EVERYTHING HERE WITH A CREDIT CARD EXCEPT FOOD??" (By the way, the rules have since changed: you *can* pay for everything with a credit card.)

I was completely geared up to deliver a tirade, as I had learned to do in France, when I noticed out of the corner of my eye that everyone in the supermarket had stopped what they were doing. They were shaking in their boots and the cringing woman behind the cash register seemed to suddenly shrink to three inches high. I woke up and remembered that I was in Canada. I looked her squarely in the eyes and proclaimed, "Well, you'll have to take a check." In my embarrassment, I flung the check in her direction and hurried out of the store.

It took me a while to see behind the niceness and realize that there is a crisis in Canada when it comes to customer service. Just as in France, there is a below-the-surface unconscious customer service philosophy reflected in how one is treated as a customer. The Canadian customer philosophy is:

"The customer is bothering me."

How can you know for sure if you are bothering your suppliers? Ask them to do something slightly outside of their normal procedure and notice the response. A sigh and "Oh, all right," is often the reluctant reply in Canada.

For over a year, every month the local phone company called our office to request that we return our long-distance telephone business to them. Every month I'd reply, "Please send me your rates and I will compare them to what we are presently getting." Every month, I was told, "We don't send information." Every month, I'd reply, "Well, you don't want me to be a customer, do you?" I suppose that sending rate information would have been a bother to them.

We asked for a quote for an event from a caterer. We were obviously bothering them because it took them two weeks to send us the information, in spite of repeated requests. Obviously we went to alternate sources. A party supplier delivered the wrong glasses for an event we hosted, and instead of apologizing and coming over with the right glasses, they informed us later that they don't operate on the weekend.

We finally got so fed up in our office that we phoned many of our suppliers and asked them, "Do you want to do business with us? If you do, we'd like you to return our phone calls and do what you commit to doing."

On a lighter note, in our office we have an ongoing competition to see who can extract the best customer service from our suppliers. We use a variety of approaches: groveling, threatening, and—escalating up the hierarchy—being very friendly or completely helpless and in need of rescuing. The winner usually figures out which approach to use based on the voice tone of the customer representative. We have found that apologizing profusely for bothering the person usually gets a positive response. Could that be because they really do believe we are bothering them? The other reason that this strategy works is that by apologizing, we are **matching the below-conscious LAB Profile Patterns of the supplier.** "Sorry for bothering you" is **moving Away From bothering them.** They then respond well to this.

The American Customer Philosophy

To people from Europe and elsewhere, Canada and the United States may seem similar. There are, however, some profound differences in culture as well as in customer service philosophies. Even though I travel frequently to the United States for both business and personal reasons, it took me a while to determine what was behind all that American enthusiasm. Canadians and Europeans do not completely understand being told to "have a great day!" when doing our shopping.

My hypothesis is that the customer service philosophy in the States is a belief about the *nature of the customer*. Here it is:

> *"The customer is a spaced-out preschooler who will not listen."*

This explains why the people serving you speak to you in a loud voice, using many gestures to point out the obvious. For example, when you take the monorail at Disney World, they have an announcement telling you to hold on, as if you did not know you were on a moving train!

This insight came to me one evening at a restaurant with a group of colleagues in Denver. I explained to my companions the thinking I had been doing on customer service philosophies in different countries and that I suspected I had just put my finger on the American philosophy. No sooner had I uttered, "The customer is a spaced-out preschooler who will not listen," than a wondrous event occurred. For perhaps the first time in my life, the universe conspired to provide evidence for a newly minted theory of mine.

Just at the moment when we were having a polite little giggle over my theory, the restaurant's customer service manager approached our table. He knelt down beside one of my dinner companions who had sent his dinner back because it was cold, stuck his face into the face of my dinner companion, and said in a very loud voice, "HI. MY NAME IS MARK. I'M THE CUSTOMER SERVICE MANAGER. MY JOB IS TO MAKE SURE THAT YOU ARE COMPLETELY SATISFIED WITH YOUR MEAL."

This is akin to the server informing you that they will be your waiter, as if you didn't know you were in a restaurant. This theory could explain why American customer service people are so enthusiastic—they are trying to hold the attention of a little person who doesn't know what is going on and is easily distracted.

Discovering Your Company's Below-Conscious Customer Philosophy

It is clear that the above customer philosophies are generalizations that do not cover every interaction. Not every customer service representative will fall under the same umbrella. Discovering your organization's customer philosophy is like doing the LAB Profile in reverse: you notice the typical behaviors, values, beliefs, and rules at play and then you can identify what Patterns are ruling the roost. Below you will find the questions to ask in order to determine the philosophy. There are several examples of how to put what you discover into LAB Profile terms. Once you know the LAB Profile of your team or organizational philosophy, you will know what language to use or avoid using when you are introducing new programs or organizational change.

Beyond cultural customer philosophies, every organization has a Below-Conscious Customer Philosophy—often one that was not intentionally chosen. Behaviors evolve, and many organizations are not even aware of the beliefs driving the behaviors of their employees.

If you want to determine the kind of philosophy driving sales and customer service in your organization or department, you will need to closely observe what people do when they are dealing with customers and ask yourself a few key questions:

- What are the employees' behaviors with the customers?
- What must these employees believe to be true to behave this way?
- If there were a philosophy, a principle, or a set of beliefs and values driving this behavior, what would they be?

Or try filling in the blank in this sentence:

■ The sales and customer service representatives are behaving as if
   _____.

Operational Values, Beliefs, and Rules

Sometimes the answers to these questions are found in the operational values: that is, those values that are evident from the behaviors you can observe. For example, does the behavior indicate who is *more important?* In a retail environment, if the customers are standing around being ignored until the sales or customer service representative feels ready to deal with them, then that implies that the representative is more important than the customer. If this is typical behavior, then the representatives are Internal with respect to the customers. They decide when they are good and ready to serve the customers.

If on the other hand, the customer service or sales representative acknowledges the presence of the customers and says when he or she will be able to serve them, it is clear that the customers have more importance than the employee. If this behavior is typical, then the representatives tend to be External to the customer and probably also have a Person Pattern, as they acknowledge the individual customers right away.

If departments operate in isolated silos, where it is a major challenge for employees to get needed input or help from another team to assist in fulfilling customer requirements, then you know that the operating values have something to do with having territory. And there is probably a fairly Procedures culture where there is a protocol for how to get things done.

Again, from observing the behavior, sometimes the answer is a belief about what is true or not true. Is the representative acting as if the customer were an idiot? This is apparent when, for example, you have taken a device in to be repaired and you are asked, "Did you plug it in?" (This does not eliminate the possibility that the customer is *in fact* an idiot, as exemplified by yours truly when complaining about products that I have been using improperly.) If the customer were asked how he or she used the product and what happened, then it is clear that the customer is being treated as if he or she is reasonable and that an investigation into what is going wrong will be undertaken.

Sometimes the answer is in a rule about what is or is not allowed. An example of this is when everyone believes they must follow the prescribed procedure: "I can't break the rules," or "It's not my responsibility." This is similar to when you were in school and the teacher said, "If I let you do it, then I'd have to let everyone else do it," as a way of saying no to a request. This is an example of an extreme LAB Profile Procedure Pattern in action. There is only one right way to do it.

It can take some time to discover the Below-Conscious Customer Philosophy in an organization. It necessitates a consistent observation of behaviors while holding the above questions regarding behaviors, beliefs, and principles in your awareness before the answer becomes obvious.

It is also clear that any customer philosophy acted out in behavior is supported by the organization or the department itself. Once you have discovered what the philosophy is, you will also have unearthed significant information about the culture of the organization.

This will help you when you decide to make improvements in customer experience, as you will know the starting point and can measure against it when you implement the changes or improvements you want to make.

The next chapters in this section will complete the picture of the major issues when responding to the Great Customer Attitude Shift: **uncovering the forces driving Customer *Outrage,* and how organizations tacitly support unproductive customer behaviors.**

CHAPTER 3

Decoding Customer OutRage

Hello. I sent my laptop computer to you for repair and just got it back. Everything that I've written on it for the past two years is gone. I was told that I'd be called if you had to replace the hard drive. I called and was told that it didn't need to be replaced. Everything that I've been working on for the past two years of my life is gone! You f---ing a--holes!

Now I want you to call me back and stop messing me around and make sure that I get back what I've been working on! Do you understand? I had better get my hard drive back or I'm going to sue all of you pieces of sh--.

LAPTOP REPAIR CALL, SUBMITTED BY SARAH AINSWORTH, UK

Even when everything goes right, customers have become difficult to deal with. They demand products and services of perfect quality, are unwilling to put up with complicated purchasing processes, and want anything that doesn't work to be fixed immediately at no cost to them. They are quick to jump on any mistakes, will give customer service staff a hard time, and will even play one supplier off another to get the best deal. They often demand more for less. And they get very angry when they don't get it.

Much has been made of this so-called "customer rage." It comes in many forms: road rage, air rage, etc. Suppliers and businesses alike are frustrated and worn out dealing with the anger of their customers. Call center staff call in sick to avoid mistreatment at the hands of angry customers. There are many examples: customers in line yelling at tellers because they had to wait more than five minutes, patients screaming at doctors' receptionists because they can't get what they want. The media has bandied about some simplistic explanations for this rage, including the demise of manners and a lack of values.

This kind of analysis has not been very helpful, as it is typically done from the perspective of the suppliers who are bearing the brunt of customers' anger. From their viewpoint, isn't someone who shouts at you unreasonable? Of course!

The Customer's Point of View

Now think about your own attitude when *you* are the customer. How do you feel when you don't get the quality or timeliness you need? What do you do when your business partners don't complete their projects when you need them? How do you react if you have to return a product that doesn't work? What goes through your mind when you try to order online and it takes forever, or it doesn't work properly? How do you feel when the doctor keeps you waiting an hour? And what about if you have been waiting in a store for some time and no one even bothers to acknowledge your presence?

Can't you feel your frustration level rising? Isn't it an *outrage* to be treated this way? When you are the customer and you want advice or need a service or product to work properly, and it isn't happening, it can be extremely annoying.

Aside from being subjected to poor service and shoddy workmanship, there are several other factors that make customers lose their cool much more quickly than before.

Shortage of Time

As everyone knows, time is in chronically short supply for many, many people. Take a look at all the activities people try to cram into their days. Those who survived the successive waves of corporate layoffs and downsizing probably noticed that while the workforce shrank, the workload did not.[1] People also don't have much unprogrammed leisure time left. If you are a woman in your 40s, for example, chances are that you work full-time while raising children and caring for at least one elderly parent. People everywhere have been trying to squeeze many more activities into a day than their parents or grandparents ever imagined. And for many people, there is an endless stream of urgent e-mail coming in second-by-second on their Blackberry or iPhone.

Any event that threatens to take too long or has to be added in poses a serious threat to one's schedule. Imagine trying to keep your cool when everyone seems to be conspiring to make you late. Stress-related illnesses have once again been increasing[2] as people try desperately to juggle all

---

[1] According to a study by the National Sleep Foundation, the average employed American works a 46-hour work week, and 38% of the respondents in their study worked more than 50 hours per week.

[2] Stress accounts for two-thirds of family doctor visits and half the deaths of Americans under the age of 65, according to the U.S. Center for Disease Control and Prevention. Studies by the American Medical Association have also shown the negative effects of stress on health. They say stress is a factor in more than 75% of all illness and disease today. Stress has been the subject of more than 20,000 scientific studies.

their commitments. No wonder more people than ever before are blowing their stack!

But time is not the only pressure faced by customers.

The Great Customer Attitude Shift

We used to tell a joke about Canadians: "How do you get 25 Canadians to get out of a swimming pool? Ask them to get out of the pool."

Those days are over, and not only in Canada! Imagine making a purchase just because you were told to by a salesperson. Or accepting the bank's first offer for a loan? Or not negotiating with your corporate suppliers over a large contract? Unthinkable, right? Many consumers make financial institutions, insurance companies, airlines, office suppliers—you name it—compete to get their business.

The Great Customer Attitude Shift has happened! Most people today are impervious to sales pitches. People now decide for themselves to purchase or not based on what is important to them. The sales pitch is mere information, grist for the mill to be compared to other offers on the table.

Allan Gregg, president of the Strategic Counsel polling organization, said, "People don't want a mortgage; they want a house. The customer does not care about how it's done or who does it. They only care about what they want."[3] He also says that what drives customers crazy is a "real inability to redress a screw-up." In the banking sector, "knows my name" is the single best indicator of satisfaction.

Decoding the Great Customer Attitude Shift

From compliant to resistant! Gone is the time when customers allowed themselves to be told what to do. The LAB Profile Patterns discussed in Chapter 1 can be used to clearly understand the shift in both motivation and behavior. For example, customers have switched from needing External direction to being Internal[4] to their suppliers. In the LAB Profile, we identify someone who needs feedback and guidance from outside sources as having an External Pattern in that situation. Someone who decides based on their own criteria and standards has an Internal Pattern.

To get a mortgage in the 1970s and earlier, customers had to beg, grovel, promise their firstborn, and agree to pay any interest rate and do

---

[3] Quote from a speech given to the Lac Carling E-government conference, April, 2007.
[4] For more detailed information on Internal and External Patterns, please see the chapter entitled "The Margaret Thatchers of the World" in my book Words *That Change Minds*.

everything the bank told them to do. In other words, customers were External to the banks: the banks demanded and customers complied.

Customers have long since been dangling the carrot of their business and watching financial institutions scramble for it. Since simple online searches and mortgage brokers have enabled consumers to get competing quotes from a wide variety of financial institutions very quickly, any institution insisting on too much time-consuming paperwork is immediately thrown out of the running. Customers did what they were told in the past, but now they have begun telling their potential suppliers what to do to get their business. When suppliers try to lay down the law, customers become offended and outraged.

The general mistrust of financial institutions was greatly exacerbated by the economic crisis that began in 2008 with the subprime mortgage collapses and subsequent government bailouts and huge executive bonuses. For quite a while, both consumers and businesses found it difficult to obtain credit in this environment, and became more compliant to bank demands. As the situation improved over time, customers reverted to being highly Internal to the banks.

Using the LAB Profile, my colleagues and I have been able to document this shift in how customers decide to purchase and how they evaluate goods and services. It shows up both in the language that customers use and in their behavior. Internal customers say things such as:

> "Send me some information and I will think about it."
> "That's not what I what. What I need is . . ."
> "You're not listening to me!"

This kind of language indicates that people are deciding for themselves based on what is important to them. They are not looking for outside guidance; they just want information and then they will make the decision. You can verbally hear the shift from External to Internal.

Normal vs. Problem Transactions: Sometimes You Just Gotta Break the Rules

Customers have one kind of behavior when their transactions are working well and a distinct set of patterns that appear as soon as a problem arises. These two sets of patterns apply both in business-to-business and business-to-consumer transactions.

Let's take another look at your relationship as a customer with your financial institution. When you make a deposit, be it online, on the phone, at a bank machine, or in person at a branch, you usually follow the bank's prescribed procedure. But what if your bank has misplaced some of your money or overcharged you for its services? The switch is instantaneous. Suddenly you are no longer willing to follow the bank's procedure—you want to find a person who will fix the problem immediately, even if they have to break the bank's standard operating procedures. If you don't get the help you want right away, you may become quite angry!

I have heard from my clients in the auto-parts industry that their customers change behavior the instant they don't get what they want. As long as each transaction was working well, the auto manufacturers were willing to follow the procedures outlined in their negotiated agreement. As soon as any issues arose, their behavior changed. If samples arrived slightly late, the screaming began at once. This behavior only became worse during the economic crisis, if they were conducting any business at all.

When the transaction is working as the customer thinks it should, customers have a LAB Profile Procedures Pattern—they just follow the normal step-by-step process. When a problem arises, customers switch to an Options Pattern. People who shift into an Options Pattern will refuse to follow the procedure. **They want all the rules broken to meet their needs.** In other words, they will not line up somewhere else and wait, they do not want to wait 45 minutes on the phone, and they certainly are not willing to e-mail a complaint—they want someone in authority to help right now!

Unfortunately, many large organizations in many fields (not just financial institutions) have not understood the precise nature of this behavior and attitude shift, nor are they sufficiently nimble in adapting to the way their customers need them to respond when a problem occurs. In fact, in a recent discussion I had with senior management at one of the largest Canadian banks, they admitted that they had a long way to go in knowing what to do when the customers got upset. And customers end up banging their heads against the wall wondering how it is possible that these companies just don't get it.

Table 3-1 details how the LAB Profile Patterns of compliant customers changed with the Great Customer Attitude Shift.

Problems occur because while many businesses have invested heavily in developing new products and services to address the change in customer behavior, **they have neglected to switch the language in which they communicate to their customers.** This is of course exacerbated during an economic crisis because customers become much more reluctant to make a buying decision and much more ready to jump down the throats of their suppliers.

TABLE 3-1 _____ **The Great Customer Attitude Shift**

Compliant Customers	Original LAB Profile Motivators	Shift in Behavior	Shifted LAB Profile Motivators	The Challenge
Do what they are told	**External** (influenced by outside factors)	Won't do what suppliers want; insist on what they want	**Internal** (decide for themselves)	Difficult to influence; skeptical
Will follow normal process	**Procedure** (follows a step-by-step method)	Insist on breaking the rules, want a special deal, individualized services	**Options** (want choices, alternatives, an exception to the rule)	Difficult to cater to individual requests
Wait for supplier to initiate or respond	**Reactive** (waiting, thinking)	Insisting, confronting, demanding	**Proactive** (taking initiative)	Difficult to predict, may become aggressive
After a few good sales or service experiences, they believe the supplier is good	**Convincer Mode: Number of Examples** (+–3, the number of positive or negative interactions needed to convince)	Each experience is evaluated separately	**Convincer Mode: Consistent** (every day is a new day; difficult to convince)	Customers believe "you are only as good as the last thing you did," no trust

Instead of offering information and inviting customers to judge for themselves—which matches the way many more customers think—companies are still touting themselves as "the best" or "the right choice." This is perceived by customers as telling them what to think and what to do. Chapters, a large Canadian book retailer, put this slogan on their bookmarks:

"You've read the reviews. Now, buy the book."

Isn't it annoying being told what to do? You have probably noticed your own increasing skepticism and impatience when you are presented with unsubstantiated claims. As a customer, do you sometimes find yourself scoffing at banks' advertising claims bragging about how much they care about you? Doesn't it raise your ire when you are told to go to another store to obtain an item listed in the original retailer's catalog? Or when you have to pay software companies for functionalities your company doesn't need?

The Emotional Charge

The other element that changes when a problem arises is the level of emotion. **Customers switch from whatever emotion is normal for them to the fight-or-flight response because they feel violated and then become outraged.** It is my belief that because customers now have firm expectations about how they want to be treated, any violation is unacceptable or intolerable. This feeling is greatly exacerbated when customers feel their supplier isn't treating the problem as seriously as they should.

Most sales and customer service representatives have been trained to stay calm when their customers express anger. Imagine that you are incensed by an incompetent mistake and your account manager says to you in a sugary voice, "Well, I can understand that you are upset." Really?! Doesn't her calm add fuel to your fire? Wouldn't you have preferred it if she were as upset by the mistake as you were?

Customer expectations have changed. Organizations are trying to change, but it is still a challenge to step outside their own frame of reference to truly understand what it is like to be a customer. Their frustration shows when they dismiss customers as "difficult" and blame customer rage on a decline in manners. They know something needs to be done, but what?

Now that the emotional and LAB Profile realities for the Great Customer Attitude Shift have been decoded, the next chapter will look at how companies reinforce the behaviors their people engage in with customers, and what to do about it.

CHAPTER 4

You Get What You Reward

Late one evening, I phoned the Internet help desk, as I was having difficulty with my product registration. I was put on hold for 45 minutes, which I had to pay for and then I finally got through. The customer service representative said cheerfully, "Hi there. How can I help?"

I replied, annoyed by my long wait, "Well, an apology for keeping me hanging on so long would be nice."

"Hmmph, I think you need to apologize to me for being so rude," she replied. "Look, I understand that it's not your fault, but I have been kept waiting and you represent the company."

She hung up on me!

ANNOYED CLIENT

Customer philosophies and behaviors, as exhibited by sales and service representatives, are supported by the organization either explicitly or implicitly. People are often directly rewarded for behaviors that may hurt customer service. One such example is when technology salespeople receive a bonus for getting contracts signed with little regard for the feasibility of actually delivering the goods. Sometimes in direct service situations, companies do not monitor what is happening, so unskilled practices and unhelpful behaviors are not corrected. How many times have you heard "This call may be monitored" with no follow-up with you, the unhappy customer?

Since many companies are unaware of the unconscious beliefs, values, rules, and LAB Profile Patterns driving their sales and service representatives' behaviors at work, this organizational support is largely indirect or implicit. In this chapter, we will uncover the ways in which organizations unwittingly foster poor customer treatment and show the LAB Profile Patterns that operate to prevent improvements.

Staffing and Staff Support

Many retail operations are chronically understaffed. This, of course, gets worse in times of low sales, where the knee-jerk reaction is to cut expenses by laying off employees. Many years ago, *Training Magazine* had a whole issue on "corporate anorexia," discussing how companies who radically cut staff can get so thin that they can't fulfill their present customers' needs.

To state the obvious, departments that are understaffed have overworked employees. It is easy to see how exhausted staff would have little patience to deal with customers.

To add to the understaffing issue, sometimes customer representatives feel they have no support from the rest of the organization. In the Canadian subsidiary of a large American manufacturer of heating systems, the customer service representatives found themselves in the untenable position of being told to lie to their customers about when their furnaces would be delivered. The problem behind the scenes was that the furnaces were manufactured in Florida, and that plant was unwilling to retool for Canadian specifications, since Canadian orders only represented 10% of their total orders. So the Canadian customer service people were told to keep delaying and making promises that management knew would not be fulfilled. I found this out after they asked me to come in to fix a "morale" problem!

The help desk people at a large American software firm had another problem. The company produced software for Health Management Organizations (HMOs) to manage health insurance claims for the employees of large organizations. When customers phoned about a glitch in the software, the help staff had great difficulty getting the operations engineers to come to their assistance. The engineers were already too busy trying to build systems and meet impossible deadlines that the sales folks had promised, therefore making their present customers a lower priority than prospective and new customers. While the cost of acquiring new customers varies widely from industry to industry, it is generally agreed that the cost of keeping and selling more to present customers is much lower than that of trying to attract new customers. So it is clearly important to keep present customers happy and coming back for more.

The above examples illustrate what happens when departmental priorities are contradictory, rather than aligned. In many of the large high-tech companies I have worked for, there are similar ingrained problems between sales and operations. Salespeople are rewarded for getting signatures on contracts. Operations people then have to deliver the services; which can leave them walking a tightrope between promises made and what can actually be done in a given time frame. Often these operations staff are the same people who are called in to do supplementary work or to fix problems after systems have been installed, which is a further drain on their time.

This kind of problem seems so obvious that many people wonder why it hasn't already been fixed. But the leadership and employees of each department are so busy trying to meet their own ambitious targets that it's difficult for them to see the larger picture and to set goals that will satisfy their clients all the way through the sales and delivery cycle.

Here are a couple of examples of how organizations implicitly encourage bad customer service.

The System Won't Allow It

I wanted to have my young son's bank account appear with my accounts online to automatically transfer his allowance to his account so that he could easily see his balance and transactions. Not possible. If his account were to be on my online account, then he would be subject to "adult" service fees instead of the no-fee youth account schedule. I argued that this didn't meet our needs. "It's the way the system is set up," was the response. I asked to speak to the head office person responsible for setting up the system, but no one knew who that might be or how to contact them. I asked for a message to be sent to the IT department, but again, they had no mechanism for doing so. It seemed logical to me that having minor children's accounts visible with the parent's accounts online would have been a useful service to many people, but there was no way to gain access to anyone with the authority to do anything about it.

There are two issues here that impact the customer. One is **that the IT department has dictated inflexible procedures and has omitted to include a system for getting feedback on how these procedures meet or don't meet customers' needs.** When this happens, it sends a clear message that IT requirements are more important than being responsive to customer needs. In LAB Profile terms, the IT function is highly Internal: they make their own decisions *based on what is important to them* and it is very difficult to influence them from the outside.

When I conduct interdepartmental mediation and conflict resolution sessions for corporate clients, this continues to be an issue. Good customer responsiveness is often sacrificed for infrastructure convenience. Conversely, from my experience working in IT, there are also many examples where IT architecture directors have difficulty getting the ear of the "C" level to invest in systems that will positively transform customer experience.

The second issue that impacts the customer is what I call the **"Front-line Customer Input Blockage."**

The Front-Line Customer Input Blockage

This second issue is more widespread; in many, many organizations there is often no mechanism for taking input from the front-line customer contact people—those who are most likely to know what the customer wants—and making sure that the key decision-makers get this information. In most of the large financial institutions and high-technology companies with which I have dealings, there isn't even a directive to solicit feedback from the front line. When I am a customer, I often get the impression that staff would rather I shut up, stop bothering them, and go home, because there is nothing they can do about my comments and helpful suggestions.

This Internal problem also exists in the health care sector. I have helped several Canadian hospital departments and one health authority in the United Kingdom rethink the communication issues in the delivery of health care services. I found myself constantly reminding the hospital about the patients. "Are they still going to have to wait hours for their appointment?" I repeated. **"How will you know, in your drive for efficiency, that you have also improved the patients' experience of dealing with your department?"** "What are your receptionists telling you about the comments they get from patients and their families?" I asked to uncomprehending stares. "Maybe it's time we found out."

The LAB Profile of Poor Customer Care

LAB Profile Patterns can help you understand and influence behaviors on the job. You can also use them to understand and change the below-conscious Motivation Triggers of your sales and service staff as well as the culture of the organization or department.

First let's describe some of the behaviors typical in poor customer care:

1. The needs of the customer are somewhat or largely ignored while the staff members focus on their own tasks.
2. No initiative is taken on behalf of the customer even when the customer is unhappy.
3. The staff members behave as if the customer is unreasonable.
4. The staff members behave as if the customer is bothering them.
5. The staff members say over and over what they can't do but offer few alternatives.
6. The staff members follow a set procedure regardless of what the customer needs or wants.

Let's decode these behaviors into some LAB Profile Pattern Motivation Triggers and Working Traits:

1. **Thing vs. Person—Staff are focusing on Things.** This means that tasks and objects are the focus of any activity, not the person.
2. **Reactive vs. Proactive—Staff are being Reactive.** There is a willingness to respond, but not initiate anything.
3. **Internal vs. External—Staff behavior responses are Internal.** Their behavior is based on the belief that anyone who doesn't fit his or her own expectations is out of line.
4. **Independent vs. Proximity vs. Cooperative—Staff working style is Independent.** They would rather work alone (or at least, *without* the customers) and seem to be disturbed by the customer.
5. **Away From vs. Toward—Staff are oriented Away From.** They are noticing only what is wrong or can't be done with regards to the customer's request.
6. **Procedures vs. Options—Staff are focused on following Procedures.** They are compelled to follow the standard process, without exception, and will not consider other alternatives (Options).

How do organizations promote these behaviors? **When there is a demand from either management or IT to focus on the completion of forms, scripts, or other bits of paper (in other words, Things, not People), with the message that there is only one right way to do transactions, you tend to get the rigid behaviors mentioned above.** Call center employees are often evaluated on whether they used the customer's name at particular times during the call and followed a rigid number of steps, rather than on whether the customer sounded satisfied or dissatisfied with the service offered.

The instructions to employees that **define the limits to action are very clear** (Procedures), while **possibilities for finding ways around problems** (Options) either have not been addressed or have been overtly proscribed. My mother reported to me that the dispatcher from her cable company was told by management that she was "not allowed" to send a repair crew in less than 24 hours, even if one was available!

Darwinian Staff Selection

The consequence of these factors is a Darwinian staff selection. Employees who are turned off by rigidly following procedures without the ability to take initiative will leave. **Those who stay internalize the rules and become highly critical of anyone who wants them to do something different.**

Chances are that if the sales and customer service employees have some of the above behaviors, they have been working for the organization for quite some time. **The ones who left after a short term might in fact be some of the ones you may want to hire in the future, if you can create an environment to support their natural inclinations.**[1]

Conflicting LAB Profiles

The collision of unhappy customers with poor customer service behaviors often creates major dramas or initiates the trickle of customers away from their suppliers. Unhappy customers shift into LAB Profile Patterns that can, in turn, run up against poor customer sales and service behaviors. And when there's a conflict, something's or someone's gotta give!

Let's look at the typical behaviors of unhappy customers:

1. They are impatient and frustrated: they'll exhibit foot tapping, big sighs, louder-than-usual voices, and large gestures.
2. They focus their attention directly at the person serving them and pay attention to everything the person says or doesn't say.
3. They don't care about rules and procedures and do not want to be made to follow them.
4. They don't want to be told what to do—this would only make them angrier.
5. They want a solution and they want it *now!*
6. Their first reaction to any proposal is skepticism and doubt, often accompanied by a rehashing of old wrongs.

If we decode these behaviors into LAB Profile Patterns, this is what we get:

1. **External vs. Internal—Customers have Internal motivation.** They know they are right in their point of view and any other perspective is wrong. They are hard to influence.
2. **Away From vs. Toward—Customer attention has become Away From.** They are focused on the perceived wrong and anything that is said or done that they do not like.
3. **Person vs. Thing—Customers are laser-focused on the Person in front of them.** They want to speak with a person who can help them now, rather than do something (Thing) such as line up over there, write to management, etc. They want someone to demonstrate that they understand the hurt caused by the problem and take care of it.

---

[1] For a great example of how a company used natural selection to create a great customer experience, see the Irish Continental case study in Chapter 13.

4. **Options vs. Procedures—An unhappy customer is not motivated to follow the supplier's procedures**. They want every rule in the book to be broken if necessary to fix the problem and insist on having alternatives (Options).

5. **Proactive vs. Reactive—The customer has become Proactive**. They want action now and they will do whatever it takes to get it. They expect that the customer service person will take whatever initiative is needed, and will do it *quickly*.

6. **Specific vs. General—For the unhappy customer, the focus is on the Specific details** of what went wrong and what needs to be done to right it. All the details of the conversations are equally important.

7. **Consistent vs. Number of Examples vs. Automatic—**Finally, the unhappy customer becomes Consistent. He is a "doubting Thomas" who is never quite convinced of the rep's or the company's good intentions or ability to come up with an answer.

When the unhappy customer with the above LAB Profile collides with poor sales or customer service behavior, communication problems can easily escalate, even without any additional organizational factors taking a part.

> Any two individuals with differing perspectives who have both become Internal will tend to assume that the other person is either wrong or unreasonable.

For the customer, this fuels the anger. For the sales representative, this adds to the belief that customers in general are difficult to deal with. Table 4-1 illustrates how this dynamic unfolds.

Both the staff member and the customer have an Away From focus, which creates in them a heightened sensitivity to anything that the other says with which they disagree. The staff person is, at the same time, focused on the task (that is, the customer's issue), which increases the likelihood that she will point out what can't be done, or why the need is impossible to meet with little regard for the customer's feelings. The customer is person-focused and skeptical, so will be staring down the rep's throat thinking what an idiot she is for not caring or being able to bend the rules to take care of a customer.

TABLE 4-1 ——————— **Conflicting Unhappy Customer and Poor Customer Service/Sales Behavior**

Unhappy Customer LAB Profile Patterns	Poor Sales/CS Behavior LAB Profile Patterns	Conflict
Internal	**Internal**	Each believes they are correct and the other is wrong.
Away From	**Away From**	Each notices what is wrong with what the other said or what won't work.
Options	**Procedures**	The customer wants alternatives while the staff member follows standard operating procedure.
Proactive (Expectations that the rep will take the initiative)	**Reactive**	The customer is likely to be a bulldozer, while the staff member becomes as passive as a child berated by a parent.
Person	**Thing**	The customer wants his/her feelings understood while the staff member focuses on the task at hand.

Companies inadvertently encourage this continued mismatch of patterns when they instruct staff to stay calm and be patient and also to refuse to tolerate rude behavior. They tell the representatives that if they stay calm, the customer will inevitably also calm down. Sometimes this works, but more often the customer leaves without getting his or her emotional or concrete needs met, and angry escalations happen frequently.

It is difficult for staff and management to take angry customers seriously when they are convinced that customers are unreasonable. The continued belief in "customer rage" prevents them from hearing the message that the customer wants them to hear. Of course, I am not condoning aggressive behavior, nor am I criticizing the need for staff to be safe in their workplace. I do believe, however, that customers become angry for a reason. It is incumbent upon service providers to capture and understand the experience clients are having and to use that information to improve what they do.

WORDS THAT CHANGE MINDS POWER PRINCIPLES

Everything you do affects the emotional state of your customer.

Everything you do determines what your customer believes about your organization.

Companies need to be able to understand the below-conscious triggers motivating their customers, and to understand how those triggers can change when the customer is unhappy. It is equally important to understand which Patterns are driving your staff, as this will be your starting point from which to make any necessary changes. Using the LAB Profile to decode these motivations and behaviors will enable suppliers to identify exactly what needs to be said and done to both solve the customer's problem and make the customer feel better. You can use the LAB Profile to determine how sales and customer service behaviors need to shift to reduce customer anger and ensure repeat business.

When organizations train and reward staff for being able to adapt to the changing needs of customers, they will reap the rewards. In the next sections, we will look at the steps for doing business in the ways your customer wants, how to solve the inevitable problems that will occur, and future-proofing your whole customer operation.

PART 3

Doing Business the Way Your Customer Wants

CHAPTER 5

Create Your Customer Philosophy to Sell More

We treat the customer like a friend. We do everything for you that we would do for a friend, including, where necessary, telling you if you are being unreasonable. Nobody is on commission here and there are no minimum sales targets built into anybody's job description. We have found them to be in conflict with good advice. Besides, most of you will spend as much money with us as you can afford so we want to give you good advice, to give you the best value and thereby guarantee ourselves a low rate of product returns. It is best for both of us if we get it right the first time around.

EXCERPT FROM LEE VALLEY TOOLS PRINCIPLES[1]

If a philosophy is a set of beliefs, then a strategy would be the plan of action for how to manifest or demonstrate those beliefs on a daily basis.

If you don't want your organization and your customers to be victims of whatever unconscious sales and service philosophies have evolved over time, it is in your best interest to make some decisions about what your philosophies will be and then to define and implement the processes necessary to make them actually happen. **This section is designed to assist you with thinking through the development of your customer sales and service philosophy to help you increase your sales.**

From Whose Point of View?

There are three main points of view[2] you may wish to consider in defining and evaluating your customer sales and service philosophy:

1. Your point of view as supplier.
2. The customer's point of view.
3. The "fly on the wall" overview perspective.

---

[1] From the Lee Valley Tools website.

[2] These three points of view are called the Perceptual Positions in Neurolinguistic Programming.

While I have seen many organizations develop what they thought would be a "customer-focused" philosophy, judging from the behavior in practice, **it was clear that they hadn't stepped out of their own point of view in order to test their ideas from the customer's perspective.** As I mentioned previously, in a leading-edge teaching and research hospital, I worked with the diagnostic imaging department to restructure the organization and delivery of radiology and other diagnostic scanning services. My role became one of reminding them, "What about the patients?" They were preoccupied with increasing their own efficiency from their point of view and neglected to check their patients' point of view.

Stepping into the customer's shoes entails remembering what it is like when *you* are purchasing goods and services. To feel like a customer, you need to *be* a customer. I suggest that you **harvest personal experiences of both bad and good service that you have received in order to create great experiences for your own customers.**

Above and beyond your point of view and the customer's point of view, there is the third position, the "fly on the wall" perspective. From this angle, you can perceive both points of view as well as the relationship between customer and supplier. Remember a time when you were listening to two people arguing and you were able to see that they were actually in *agreement*, although neither was aware of it?

This third position gives you an overview. **From here, you will be able to evaluate more objectively the consequences of your carefully developed Customer Philosophy and your resulting Customer Care Process.** For instance, if what the customer wants is the priority, are there limits on what a staff member can authorize? Lee Valley Tools empowered each staff member to refund a customer up to the total amount the customer had paid if the customer was not happy about something. Focusing on these three positions as you develop or enhance your Customer Philosophy will ensure that your people create great experiences for your customers.

Components of a Sound Customer Philosophy

Consider the following as you develop your Customer Sales and Service Philosophy:[3]

- Spirit
- Atmosphere
- Beliefs

---

[3] These categories are inspired by Robert Dilts' work on Neuro-Logical Levels. For more information, see Robert Dilts & Judith Delozier, *Encyclopedia of Systemic NLP*, NLP University Press, 2000, pp. 866–868.

- Goals
- Standards to be met
- Automatic feedback processes
- Triggers of change mechanisms

Below are some questions to debate for each component. As you work through each, first take your customers' experience as your primary point of view,[4] then check from your own (supplier's) viewpoint to ensure feasibility, and finally use the fly-on-the wall overview to make sure your own system makes sense.

Spirit

What is the soul of the organization that you want to communicate to your customers? Generosity? Integrity? Caring? Knowledgeable? Elite? Unique? Responsive? Innovative? What would be well received by your customers or potential customers? Describe the essence of your organization.

Atmosphere

What is the environment you want to create when your customers enter your space? Welcoming? Homey? Professional? Friendly? Efficient? Rigorous? What qualities match both your customers' conscious and below-conscious desires and expectations, as well as the spirit of your organization? How will your physical environment reflect this?

Beliefs

What do you or will you believe about your customers? Are they intelligent? Do they contact you because they are troubled? Because they have a problem? Because they have an objective? Because they need help figuring out what their objective ought to be? Who do your customers believe they are? Patients? Consumers? Volunteers? Researchers? Knowledgeable? Uninformed but searching for knowledge? How would you describe the customers you have and want to attract? Consider age, values, beliefs, behavior, problems, and goals. Are your customers in a hurry, or would they like to browse? What evidence do you have to confirm or challenge these beliefs?

---

[4] You can base your philosophy on your customers' expectations and desires by conducting LAB Profile customer research; see Chapter 12. For another great example of how to determine expectations and desires, try my CD/MP3 program *Building Long Term Relationships with Clients: Decode What They Really Want*, available from www.WordsThatChangeMinds.com.

What do you want your customers to believe about your organization? That you are trustworthy? Responsive? Reliable? Friendly? Fun? Efficient? Quirky?

What do you want the general public to believe about your organization?

A major pharmaceutical company hired my company to take our customer care program across the country to retail pharmacists. We made a surprising discovery as we spoke to both pharmacists and the people who use the services of pharmacies. While the pharmacists believed that they were dealing with patients, these "patients" had no idea that they were patients. They thought they were "customers." The way one treats a patient is very different from how one treats a customer.

Goals

Given the spirit, atmosphere, and beliefs you decided on, what are your specific goals for sales and customer service, in terms of the experience you want your customers to have? Would you like your clients to be accompanied through a decision process from beginning to end? Or do you want your salespeople not to interfere with the customers' desire to explore, but just be around to help when needed? Should the product options be clearly visible from anywhere in a retail environment, or is there a progressive, step-by-step mechanism to help people find what they want (LAB Profile Procedures)? (This is a relevant question for both retail and online shopping.) Do you wish to provide your clients with many ways to do business (LAB Profile Options)?

Standards

How will you know that you are doing business in the right way? In a way that reflects the spirit, atmosphere, beliefs, and goals you have developed? What are your criteria for knowing that you are doing a good job at customer care? What staff and customer behaviors will be valued and rewarded? Will you reward staff for numbers of customers served per hour or some other standard?

Automatic Feedback Mechanisms

How will you know if your standards are being met, or even if they are the correct standards to have? How will you continually gather information about your customers' experience of doing business with you, without bothering them? How will you judge this—from customer feedback

(LAB Profile External) or from in-house measurements (LAB Profile Internal)? What behaviors from staff and customers will indicate that you are on- or off-track? How will you sort and interpret this information? From what point of view (yours, your customers', or the fly-on-the-wall perspective) will you analyze the data? How will you recognize important patterns? And lastly, how will you communicate back to staff and customers about the feedback you get from them and the actions you have taken as a result? Do you invite input from your customers?

Allan Gregg, the well-known pollster, says there needs to be a "constant feedback loop between customers and providers; a constant process communication to tap into the common wisdom of men and women."[5]

Here is an invitation to customers from Lee Valley Tools on their website:

> We listen. If you want us to change something or to carry another product, let us know; we may not end up doing what you want but we won't ignore your comments. We have had a lot of good advice from customers over the years and appreciate it. We also get some bad advice; the trick always is in being able to tell which is which, something we are still working on.

Triggers of Change Mechanisms

At what point will you adjust your sales and customer service philosophy, strategy, and processes? How many times does a problem or unsatisfactory situation have to occur before you will reexamine the system/process in order to find a solution and prevent it from happening in the future? What is the earliest point at which to make adjustments without throwing the whole system into chaos? How will you distinguish between an isolated event and an indicator of an underlying problem? How many examples of something not working will it take to trigger a re-examination or modification?[6]

Or will you behave like the British bank in this incident?

> A client phoned the bank to request changing the date on which her loan payment was to be deducted from her account. The customer service representative replied that this change of date would not be possible. "How can you be so certain that it is not possible?" asked the customer. "I'm quite certain," said the customer service representative, "because we've had many people ask us to do it. That's how I know it can't be done."
>
> OVERHEARD IN A BANK

---

[5] Excerpt from a speech given to the Lac Carling E-government conference, April 2007.

[6] See Chapter 14 for more information on how to implement Automatic Feedback Mechanisms and Triggers of Change Mechanisms as part of providing a customer experience that is congruent with your branding.

Success Strategies' Customer Philosophy

My business is certainly different than yours, but here is an example of how we answered the above questions in developing our LAB Profile Consultant/Trainer Certification Program. The program is designed to build the necessary skills to make advanced use of the LAB Profile in leadership, sales, marketing, and learning programs. Each year business leaders, marketers, trainers, consultants, and coaches come from around the world to attend this learning program. Here is our Customer Philosophy:

Spirit

Generosity, both personal and professional. We will do the maximum before, during, and after the program to make sure participants have what they need to be physically and emotionally comfortable, learn what they need to learn, and be able to create a successful business using the LAB Profile.

Atmosphere

Welcoming, professional yet friendly, rigorous, and elite. This learning experience is a profoundly unique time in participants' lives where they are guided through a process to stretch their creative, intellectual, and improvisational abilities through exercises and concise feedback.

Beliefs

The people who participate have a complex and somewhat contradictory relationship with us. They are both customers and students. They are purchasing training from us and, at the same time, being evaluated by us. Sometimes they demand services as if they were customers; at other times, they request guidance as a student would from a teacher. They are adults, capable of taking care of their own needs and requesting help or information when they cannot find what they are looking for.

This is a training event, not a conference. For us, this awareness came over time. For the first year we treated it like a conference, where every logistical arrangement was handled by us for our participants: transportation to and from the airport, hotel reservations, car rental, etc. The result was that many participants viewed us as responsible for everything, including their moods. When we changed our belief to "This is a 'training event' where participants are adults," the whining stopped and people took care of their own needs and logistics. We got much more positive feedback as well, since taking care of others' needs correctly is more difficult than letting them do it themselves. (Try to get agreement on menu choices and room temperature or a million other details!)

Goals

Our customer goals are:

1. To anticipate and fulfill participants' needs with regards to information (pre-course assignment, how to meet certification standards) and continually improve with regards to effective use of resources to meet participants' needs;
2. To notice participants' reactions to the learning processes designed and the logistics we put in place and look for ways to improve their experience through design;
3. To make it easy for participants to give us spontaneous feedback and suggestions by having staff available for conversation during the breaks and learning sessions; and
4. To consider feedback and suggestions received, make decisions, and communicate our decisions with the participant or whole group, if appropriate.

Standards

The following indicate whether we have succeeded in creating the spirit, atmosphere, beliefs and goals we want to create for our customers:

1. Participants spontaneously comment on the excellent quality of learning, on how responsive we are as well as how clear we are on our expectations of them.
2. Participants say we have been helpful and supportive to them as they are learning.
3. Participants make suggestions to improve the experience and/or notice things that are out of place or not helpful.

Automatic Feedback Mechanisms

Prior to commencement of the program, we will note the questions participants ask and check our process for delivering the information to see if it can be improved. The questions customers ask are often an indicator of whether or not the information was conveyed in a way that people can easily get it and retain it. More people prefer an overview to reading de-tailed information, and this can be a handicap if you need your customers to be very well informed. Summaries can help this problem, as can an easy-to-access online portal so they can refresh their memories as needed.

During the program, each coach of the end-of-day Integration Groups will gather information on questions or suggestions the participants have and will make note of the emotional state of participants.

Triggers of Change Mechanisms

One negative comment will make us check what we are doing. Several will provoke a change. We can afford to do this as we are a very small enter-prise. One year we had a couple of comments on the quality of the video we sent people as part of their pre-course assignment. Apparently the sound quality was not good in parts. We redid the video and made sure it was of excellent quality, since, for our customers, it reflected on the per-ceived "quality" of what we offer.

While this is probably impractical for larger organizations, our trig-ger of change is "One-Trial Learning That is, we will review a process when we receive one negative comment in order to determine how to pre-vent that problem from reoccurring. If we were to wait until we received three or four similar negative comments about something, it might be too late. From the perspective of our customers, if there is an issue that is suf-ficiently important that they take the time to tell us about it, we owe it to them to do something about it quickly and to communicate our actions to them. There were probably many others who felt the same way, didn't tell us, and probably thought less of us for it. We incorporate their comments, change what needs changing, and thank them for "putting a flea in our ear" about it.

When I posted a new article on my blog called "**The Motivation First-Aid Kit,**" I received a comment a few weeks later. The customer said that she thought the article was excellent and she had passed it on to her boss, who also liked it very much, but they could not pass it to other managers because there were too many typos in the text. I leaped into action, cor-rected the mistakes, and re-sent the article to her with my profound thanks for pointing them out to me. She replied:

> "I sent the corrected version to my team, and suggested you were an exam-ple of the graceful recovery that we have been discussing in our meetings. Thanks Shelle."

These are the key elements of a sound customer philosophy. They en-sure that you create systems that will encourage and support your customers as they go through the process of deciding to do business with you and continuing to give you their business. The next step is to ensure the quality of that experience at each moment of contact. The way to do that is to have a well-defined customer process.

The Case for a Customer Process

Customers interact with their suppliers through many channels: in person, by phone, online, in chat, etc. In my experience working with organizations on their customer issues, I have come across many organizations that either have not defined a customer process for any channels or have a process in place for some channels but not others. Even though there may be a great deal of customer *outrage*, many organizations have failed to create a process or set standards for how customers are to be treated. Often the customers are at the mercy of the moods of customer service and sales staff. I recently commented to a salesperson in a high-end leather shop on how busy it was and she replied, "Yep. It's too much. I'm exhausted." I thought, but did not say, "At least this way, you have a job!" and "Would your boss be as upset as you that there are so many customers?"

Why bother having your sales and customer service representatives follow a process when dealing with your customers? Organizations that have such processes know that the benefits are many:

- Ensuring that staff or the automatic channels handle customers properly
- Avoiding forgetting messages you want them to relay
- Having the means in place for dealing with unhappy customers
- Gathering critical information from customers about what they want and don't want

From the staff point of view, a process:

- Specifies what they are supposed to do
- Enables them to perform with assurance and confidence
- Gives them a clear mandate for action

For the customer, having someone who knows what they are supposed to be doing is reassuring—unless, of course, the staff member rigidly and mechanically goes through steps the customer feels are unnecessary.

Having a customer process facilitates the recruitment and training of new employees, saving time and costs for getting them up and running. The process itself needs to be clear regarding what needs to be done when, and should give the latitude necessary to match the needs of individual customers. In Chapters 6 and 7, I will discuss the processes an organization needs to set up to handle both normal and problem transactions with customers and after-sales service issues.

When an organization has a well-designed philosophy and a clear-cut customer process, both customers and staff feel well taken care of and are more likely to get their needs met on many levels. It's like having a footpath to follow. These tools also prevent recurring issues from harming an organization, since they incorporate feedback and evidence-based information into the continual improvement of the organization and its service delivery.

CHAPTER 6

The Words That Change Minds
Customer Transaction Process

| *1. Greeting* | *2. Needs* | *3. Knowledge* | *4. Nourish* |
| *and Rapport* | *Determination* | *and Solutions* | *the Relationship* |

The workers were all set to lay my ceramic tile. The day before they were to come, I spent some time looking at the tile that was to go around my fireplace—but something was terribly wrong. They were not the color I had chosen when I had ordered them six weeks earlier. To make matters worse, there were tiny, dirty-looking scratches all through them: an "aging effect," I figured. I realized that I couldn't live with them and desperately wondered where I could find tile that I could pick up right away. I wasn't prepared to create another delay in our construction project.

I canvassed three tile stores and found nothing in stock that would do. In the fourth store, I found a busy clerk who was answering three phones at once. She smiled at me while talking to a phone customer, winked, and whispered that she'd only be a minute. I mouthed "tile" to her and she passed me a catalog and pointed to where the displays were. She was with me two minutes later, profusely apologizing for having been longer than expected on the phone. When I explained my urgent need for the right tile, she looked very thoughtful. Then she grilled me on the colors and styles of my walls and furniture as well my preferences. With that information in hand, she rapidly flipped through the catalog and put a call into inventory to check which numbers were in stock.

Then I found the tile I wanted. She checked but none were in stock. "Wait a minute," she said, and put a phone call in to their warehouse 40 minutes away. "I can't get it for you today, but they promised me it'll go on the truck tomorrow morning to get here by the afternoon. Can you live with that?" I decided I could indeed live with a one-day delay to get the tile I wanted. She then showed me some beautiful decorative tiles to create an accent around my fireplace—and went to the warehouse to pick them up for me. I was so amazed with her treatment that I went to see her boss immediately to ask him to give her a raise.

This sales representative had her priorities in order. She had a process to ensure that the customer's needs were met at each moment even if she was too busy to be there each step of the way. That's what this chapter is all about; how to guarantee that you manage your customers' experience throughout their contact with your organization.

Words That Change Minds: Customer Transaction Process

Having taken a look at the interaction between customers and suppliers from the customer's, the supplier's, and the fly-on-the wall perspective, I developed a four-step process to **enable sales and customer service staff to quickly and easily meet customers' practical and emotional needs.** The goal of this process is to establish and maintain a positive relationship with your customers, and to make sure they want to keep doing business with you.

The philosophy behind this approach is based on the Words That Change Minds Power Principles:

Everything you do affects the emotional state of your customer.

Everything you do determines what your customer believes about your organization.

Customer retention is often largely based on the relationship you establish while meeting customers' needs.[1] Effective sales processes have long ago shifted their focus from *"selling the customer"* to *"helping the customer buy."* Your organization may be doing much of this already. If so, the four steps outlined in Table 6-1 and discussed below can serve as a checklist to make sure that you have covered all the fundamentals.

---

[1] Tom DeWitt & Michael K. Brady, **"Rethinking Service Recovery Strategies: The Effect of Rapport on Consumer Responses to Service Failure,"** *Journal of Service Research*, Vol. 6, No. 2, 193–207 (2003). Four independent studies indicated that having an existing rapport between the customer and service provider reduced the number of failures to satisfy the customer's needs, decreased negative word-of-mouth, and also increased customer satisfaction and repatronage intentions.

TABLE 6-1

TABLE 6-1 ─── **Words That Change Minds Customer Transaction Process: Overview**

1. Greeting and Rapport	2. Needs Determination	3. Knowledge and Solutions	4. Nourish the Relationship
Make customer feel welcome.	Ensure you understand what they need/want.	Provide expertise to meet the need.	Create a positive relationship for next time.

1. Greeting and Rapport[2]

Greeting customers is about how you set up a relationship with them from the moment they enter your company's space, be it in person, over the phone, or even how they are welcomed on your website. Rapport is the skill required for getting on the same wavelength with someone quickly and easily. This first step enables you to plan the kind of experience you want your customers to have.

Customers need immediate acknowledgment that you know they are there. Make sure the front-line staff lets them know who will be taking care of them. When they are not acknowledged, they may quickly shift to impatience and sometimes rage. Once they reach that stage, satisfying their needs becomes more difficult.

Use something I call the **Special Event Tone** to indicate that dealing with the customer is in fact a special event. It is special for the client, and your front-line staff or call center people can reflect the importance of the event by having it show up in their tone. Use a voice tone of quiet enthusiasm (a challenge to describe in a book!).

Rapport is essentially about how one demonstrates understanding and respect for the client. One gets into rapport by matching the client's:

- Behavior (nonverbal)
- Values and key words (what is important to the client)
- Representation systems (how the client thinks)

It is the bus stop scenario again. Remember that to establish rapport, you need to meet the customer at their bus stop. Most people are naturally good at establishing rapport, but doing this with someone you don't know or with whom you are speaking for the first time can be a challenge. While getting into rapport with a friendly client may be easy, cre-

---

[2] The idea of establishing rapport by reflecting back a person's values, nonverbal behavior, and Representation Systems was developed by the creators of Neuro-Linguistic Programming (NLP), Richard Bandler and John Grinder.

ating rapport with an angry or impatient customer takes skill and prac-tice. The key skill is being able to match what the customer is experienc-ing and communicating.

Matching Behavior[3]

People who are in rapport tend to match each other in posture, gestures, and eye contact. (Note, however, that direct eye contact may not be ac-ceptable in some cultures.) The deeper the rapport, the closer the match. To create rapport, match the other person's body language with respect and sensitivity. Establishing rapport allows you to break it later when it is time to say goodbye.

What to match:

- Voice tone, timbre, speed
- Physical behavior, gestures
- Facial expression

Tips

- Acknowledge presence of customer
- Greet all clients within 15–20 seconds of arrival or sooner. For example:

"Good morning/afternoon."
"I will be with you as soon as I can."

As an example, when dealing with long lines in retail environments:

- Establish eye contact with each person in line to acknowledge their presence
- Greet with an explanation: *"It's really busy in here today; I'm going to get to each one of you as soon as I can."*
- Give a realistic time expectation if the wait may be long

Matching Criteria, Values, and Key Words

What exactly are criteria, values, and key words?

- Words associated with something important to the person
- Hot buttons—they are actually linked to feelings
- Words that cause an emotional reaction
- Words that can have a positive or negative connotation for the person
- They can mean something different for each person

---

[3] This information comes from the Neuro-Linguistic Programming field.

Similar to matching posture, gesture, and eye contact, repeating back a person's values and key words tells them you have heard them and have understood their situation.

Tips

- People will *mark out* important words with their voice tone and/or gestures
- When people *repeat* themselves, they are indicating their belief that you didn't hear or understand them
- People will usually stop repeating themselves when you play back their key words, because then they *know* you have understood

Representation Systems

Customers will give you information about not only what they are thinking, but also how they are doing this. Some people process information by seeing it in their mind's eye, some by hearing an internal dialogue, and others by sensing things physically or emotionally.

Seeing

These customers will **show you** what they are thinking. They **paint pictures** in their words; they want to **see** to understand; they like to **visualize** and may ask you to **clarify** the deal. They will **imagine** in their **mind's eye** what you are talking about. You can recognize these people easily because they use words such as **see; look; show; perspective; image; clear; clarify; light; dark; shiny; colorful; visualize; light up; vague; foggy; horizon; flash**.

Hearing

These customers like to **talk** and **listen** to what is being **said**. They place great importance on what **sounds right** to them. **Answering their questions** using "hearing language" will ensure that you have **tuned into** what they want. They use words such as **hear; talk; listen; wonder; say; question; ask; dialogue; ring; noise; rhythm; tune; harmonious; musical; tone; discord; symphony; shout**.

Sensing

These customers may speak slower than the above customers because they are processing information by **feeling**, both **physically** and **emotionally**.

They need to have a positive **gut feeling** about what they buy and will want to make sure they have a **good hold** on the information. You can recognize them because they may say things such as **sense; feel; touch; grasp; gather; in contact with; connect; concrete; pressure; sensitive; solid; closed; open; soft; hurt; link; hot; cold; warm; near.**

When you are first meeting a new prospective customer or serving someone who has done business with you, you can match your vocabulary to theirs. I'm sure that you **see** what I mean—that there is no **discord** for you in this idea and it makes good **sense.**

The Retail Environment

Greeting customers in a retail environment requires knowing the fine line between being present and pouncing on your customer like a starving tiger smelling meat. If you have hired Proactive salespeople and you pay them commission, they are often too aggressive for those customers who are browsing and don't want help. On the other hand, very Reactive retail staff members may find it difficult to make themselves available when the customer wants to talk to them. I once found myself jumping up and down in front of the counter in a large electronics store in an effort to get the associate to look up from his computer screen and acknowledge my presence.

I developed a particularly Canadian strategy for retail salespeople walking this fine line between helpful and aggressive. It entails looking toward the client, stepping back, and making a comment about the weather.[4] This will put you in rapport with most Canadians. For other cultures, there are probably safe topics of conversation that you can use to avoid the dreaded "Can I help you?" "No, I'm just looking" interaction.

2. Needs Determination

People often have several levels of needs when they contact your organization. Sometimes salespeople have to dig in order to determine the customer's actual desired outcomes. Customers frequently arrive convinced that they want a certain thing: a specific solution. The challenge can become extracting from them what the problem or the goal really is, in order to verify that they have chosen the right solution. Sometimes they don't know what they want or need, but are well aware of the existing problem.

---

[4] Culture alert! If you want to get into rapport with Canadians, whine about the weather and the price of gasoline. See my article "Whining and Connection Theory." on my website: www.Words ThatChangeMinds.com.

In each organization and type of business, there are typical reasons that people need customer service. In banks, for example, many customers simply want to complete a transaction. In the health care sector, patients want help solving a medical problem or coordinating care. In retail, they may be browsing, looking for ideas, or comparing prices, while at other times they are ready to purchase. On websites, many people simply want to access information and need it presented in a specific way. In business-to-business transactions, customers may need information, expertise, or solutions. If you can predict the specific needs your customers have when they enter your space, you can preplan how to meet and exceed their expectations. The following strategies can help you determine what a customer really needs.

After greeting the customer and taking a reading on their mood, the next step is to find out what they want. Sales and customer service representatives can use the **Funnel Question** strategy by starting with open-ended questions and gradually narrowing down to the essentials. **Summarize the client's request, using their key words to check that you have understood.** If they have other information to add, they will probably do it at this time. Staff need to verify that they have gotten out everything the customer needs. To ensure this, they can try:

> "So you want to make sure that you get the report from the tests?"

> "You need to ensure the orders arrive within three days?"

Tip

If a person shares a problem that they are having, listen and show empathy. Make every effort to empathize with the person, not the problem. (If you see the problem the same way as the client, you may not be able to find a solution.)

This means demonstrating that you understand how inconvenient the problem may be, but avoid agreeing that the problem is unsolvable. My customers have told me many stories about how difficult it is to get their teams to embrace change, to have a different attitude with respect to clients. My response is to acknowledge the frustration and to hint that there is in fact a solution:

> "Isn't it frustrating that they haven't yet gotten on board! (Wait for response) Sometimes that happens because they perceive the changes to be negative from their perspective and need to hear it or get it in a different way."

3. Knowledge and Solutions

After establishing rapport and understanding your client's needs, your next step is to prove your worth to the customer by sharing your expertise, suggesting solutions, and offering insight.

How Many Options?

How do you decide the number of options to offer your clients? If you do not know their LAB Profile preference—Options (wants lots of choices) or Procedures (prefers a clear-cut process to follow rather than many choices)—the ideal solution is to offer two or three choices. This allows the person to choose without overwhelming a Procedures person with too much choice.

Handling Questions

You want to ensure that you have thoroughly answered your customer's questions without taking all day to do it.

First, check that you have understood the question:

"You want to know whether . . . [customer's key words]?"

Secondly, make sure that you have established your credibility before you answer:

"In my experience . . ."

Thirdly, it is recommended to **make suggestions rather than telling clients what to do.** If your ideas are perceived as commands, customers may not be as open to them. They will be more apt to consider them if they are presented as suggestions.

You may wish to try out using the **Language of Suggestion**, as for Internal people as opposed to **Command Language** (which works better with External people), to make sure that you do not offend clients by appearing too bossy. For example:

"You may wish to . . . "

"I suggest that . . . "

"You may want to consider . . . "

4. Nourish the Relationship

How do you wrap up a customer transaction and ensure that you have left a positive taste in your customer's mouth so that they want to do more business with you? How do you get people to finish up when they really want to tell you their life story? How can you check that you have met their needs and make sure they know it too? What is different for phone, in-person, and website interactions?

Imagine that the phone continues to ring or there are people waiting impatiently in line. Ending an exchange while maintaining a good relationship is as important as starting it. When your customer called or visited, you had a new opportunity to influence how they felt and what they believed to be true about you and your organization. Now that you are about to send them away, here's your chance to make serving them easier next time.

Verify You Have Met Their Needs

"Did you get everything you needed about . . . [customer's key words]?"

Be Reassuring

Let them know that they can count on you and everyone else in the organization when they need assistance.

Tips

- To get off the phone when you have met the client's needs but the person wants to continue talking, wait for them to pause or take a breath, and ask:

    "So that's everything for you today, Mr. Lee?"
    "Is there anything else I can get for you, Mrs. Pa?"
    "Is that everything you needed?"

- Or try to watch timing. For example, just before they start a new topic, use an apologetic tone and state:

    "I wish I could talk to you longer, Miss Coglin . . ."

- If all else fails, have a short coughing fit and then say:

    "Please excuse me. Will there be anything else, Jocelyn, or is that it for now?"

In order to set up the future with your client, create a positive image in your customer's mind about any future experience they may have with your organization:

"The next time you have a question, you can either pick up your phone or walk into the store and any of us here can give you a hand."

End the process by shifting your voice tone to signal the end of the conversation.

TABLE 6-2

Customer Transaction Process Skills and Techniques

1. Greeting and Rapport	2. Needs Determination	3. Knowledge and Solutions	4. Nourish the Relationship
Special Event Tone	**Funnel Questions**	Explain next steps: **Procedure Language** with **Information Tone**	Check if there is anything else.
Rapport: Match client's inflection, speed of speech, and key words	**Curiosity Tone** **Summarize** what client wants	Get **Permission** to make suggestions	Say thanks with **Grateful Tone**
	Repeat Client's Key Words	When appropriate, offer **two Solutions** to give client choice	"Anyone here would be delighted to help," use **Reassuring Tone**
	Get agreement ("Is that right?")	Use the **Language of Suggestion** and the **Here's Why Approach**	Create a **visual image** in the client's mind of **future positive experiences**
		Ask which solution client prefers	
		Double Check to verify client is okay with solution using **Client's Key Words**	

Words That Change Minds Customer Communication Techniques

1. **Rapport:** Match client's tone, inflection, and speed of speech to get on the same wavelength with the client from the first few words.
2. **Funnel Questions:** Start with open questions and gradually narrow down to the essential.
3. **Client's Key Words:** Words and phrases stressed or repeated to indicate importance.

TABLE 6-3 **Words That Change Minds Phone Tones**

Name of Tone	Purpose	Description	Desired Response
Special Event Tone	To let the client know this conversation is special to you too	Quiet enthusiasm	Client becomes more enthusiastic
Curiosity Tone	To show you are interested	Tone up on the end of sentences	Client gives you the information you need
Information Tone	To provide information in a credible way	Keep tone even, credible, monotone, down at end of sentences	Client believes what you say
Grateful Tone	To show appreciation for the client's patronage	Warm tone, emphasis on "you" in "thank *you*"	Client becomes warm and friendly
Reassuring Tone	To set up a positive experience for the next time the client needs to call	Comforting, friendly	Client expresses appreciation

4. **Procedure Language:** List first step, second step, and last step, so the customer knows that you know what to do.
5. **Two Solutions:** Offer two options so the client gets to decide while you are still giving them guidance. (Fits for people with either Options or Procedures preferences.)
6. **Language of Suggestion:** Propose and offer rather than tell.
7. **Double Check:** Repeat a decision to give the client the chance to express any doubts or re-affirm the choice, using the client's key words.
8. **Permission:** Ask if it's all right before moving on to ensure agreement.
9. **Here's Why Approach:** Explain the benefits and problems solved by choosing each of the solutions.
10. **Nourish the Relationship:** Create a visual image in the client's mind of future positive experiences with your organization. Invite the client to call again any time they need something. This sets up a positive expectation for future contacts. Reassure the customer that they will be well cared for each time.

Normal vs. Problem Transactions

The above process outlines what is a "normal transaction" with a customer. It is effective for everyday sales and service transactions, where the interaction is relatively straightforward. Organizations that excel have people who know enough to ask one or two extra questions to determine what the customer really needs and to pay attention to every step of the customer interaction. The Access Center for the Regional Municipality of Halton is an excellent example of this. Their front-line staff members aim to provide the vast majority of information to residents who call the regional government; they do this by inquiring why a client is looking for something. This allows them either to give them the correct information right away or direct them to the appropriate person.

However, when the customer has a problem or is upset, many organizations lack the flexibility needed to switch modes to deal with the emotional customer. Front-line sales and customer service staff are often left to fend for themselves when customers are annoyed, relying on skills they may have learned themselves, without much direction from their organizations.

The Customer Is Bothering Me is designed to give you processes for both normal and problem interactions, based on the below-conscious motivations for each of these kinds of transactions. We'll look at problem transactions in depth in Part 4 and give some solid steps and suggestions on how to succeed in even the most difficult customer situations.

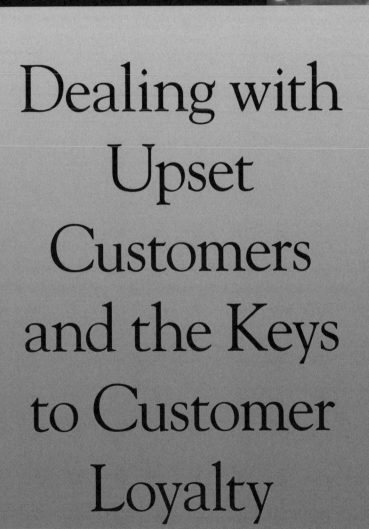

Dealing with Upset Customers and the Keys to Customer Loyalty

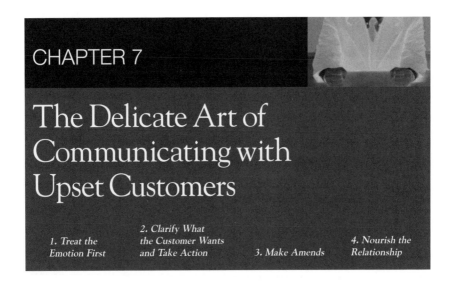

CHAPTER 7

The Delicate Art of Communicating with Upset Customers

| 1. Treat the Emotion First | 2. Clarify What the Customer Wants and Take Action | 3. Make Amends | 4. Nourish the Relationship |

"Every customer complaint represents a chance to correct a flawed process, educate a customer, and strengthen loyalty. But unless management can quantify the return on investment of complaint handling, they won't see the link between complaint handling and loyalty and profits. A process improvement in complaint handling can move customers from dissatisfied to satisfied without extra expense."[1]

According to John Goodman, 50% of consumers will complain about a problem to a front-line person. In business-to-business environments, 75% of customers will complain to a front-line person.

Upset customers want alternatives now. Your interaction with an upset customer is crucial. How the situation is resolved can determine whether they begin to think about transferring their business to other suppliers. Banks and other financial institutions know that unhappy customers don't tend to close all of their accounts at once, but rather open one account at another institution and gradually move their business over, making this slow trickle hard to detect. The Words That Change Minds Upset Customer Process demonstrates the steps to quickly calm an angry customer and create positive experiences and return clients. First we'll look at the LAB Profile of upset customers, and then I'll introduce you to the Upset Customer Process, which will be illustrated in more detail in the subsequent chapters in this section. The Upset Customer Process can be used to defuse any explosive situation either at work or in one's personal life.

---

[1] John Goodman, *Quality Progress*, Vol. 39, No. 2, February 2006, pp. 28–34.

Research shows that fixing problems quickly is good for business. Customers appreciate quick attention when something goes wrong.[2] When you have a system in place for handling upset customers your staff can identify and resolve issues easier, there are fewer escalations to management, and you are likely to satisfy your clients more, simply because you took their complaints seriously. Employee satisfaction is also higher when staff know what to do and feel confident in how to handle upset customers and complaints.

The Words That Change Minds Upset Customer Process is a four-step process that not only treats the present problem, but also re-creates a positive relationship for the future. It is separate and distinct from the normal transaction process. Staff can be taught when to switch to the Upset Customer Process.

In this chapter, we will give you an overview of the process. Each of the subsequent chapters will explain in detail how each step works and the techniques and skills involved. The Upset Customer Process is a great way to handle conflicts and other disputes in any situation.

The Words That Change Minds Influencing Principles of meeting customers at their bus stop take on even more weight when you are dealing with upset customers.

To get someone to go somewhere with you, you need to meet them where they are, and not just pretend they're already where you want them to be.

BUS
STOP

Meet them at their bus stop.

Again, remember that everything you do affects the emotional state of the customer and that your organization's or staff's actions—or inactions, for that matter—determine how the customer perceives your organization as a whole.

The Words That Change Minds Upset Customer Process enables you to go to the bus stop where your customers are. Invite them to get on the bus from their bus stop, and then bring them to a much happier place.

---

[2] Ninety-five percent of customers whose problems were resolved quickly stated they would buy again from their supplier. John Goodman's first finding, published in 1988, is that customers who complain and are satisfied are up to 8% more loyal than if they had no problem at all. This behavior has since been observed across all types of products and services. Source: John Goodman, TARP. These numbers continue to be confirmed by more recent studies.

To these important concepts we also add a truth that most people already know deep down:

THE WORDS THAT CHANGE MINDS PROBLEM-SOLVING PRINCIPLE

Human beings cannot be emotional and logical at the same time.

If they are upset, you need to deal with the emotions first and then the problem.

There is no point in helping a customer with a problem while that customer is in a negative emotional state. When someone is upset, they are busy feeling their emotions and cannot take in information at the same time. They cannot hear what you are saying until you prove that you have heard them.

The LAB Profile Patterns of Upset Customers

The Words That Change Minds Upset Customer Process is based on understanding the LAB Profile Patterns of upset customers and what they need in order to calm down and help solve the problem. Table 7-1 lays out the typical LAB Profile for an upset customer and their expectations and behaviors.

On the receiving end of this aggressive behavior are the sales and customer service representatives. **Unfortunately, most of them have been trained to stay calm when their customers are seething.**

The problem with staying calm is that the customer may believe:

- **Problems are the normal way of doing business in your organization**
- **No one does anything about problems**
- **You've heard it all before**
- **You don't care**
- **The organization doesn't care about its customers**

At a below-conscious level, when you do not acknowledge and show respect for the customers' emotional state, the customers believe you are not acknowledging them as people.

One day, while speaking to a client about the keynote speech I was about to give to his group of employees, I mentioned my Upset Customer Process, and why it was so important to go to the customer's emotional bus

TABLE 7-1 ———————————— **The LAB Profile of Upset Customers**

LAB Profile Patterns	Upset Customer LAB Profile Patterns	Expectations and Behaviors
Source: Internal vs. External	Internal	Decides for themselves; hard to influence.
Direction: Away From vs. Toward	Away From	Notices what is wrong with what the other person says or ideas that won't work.
Stress Response: Feelings vs. Choice vs. Thinking	Feelings	Stuck in a highly negative emotional state; volatile behavior.
Reason: Procedures vs. Options	Options	Wants alternatives and willing to break rules to get what they want.
Level: Reactive vs. Proactive	Proactive expectations (that the rep will take initiative)	Likely to be a bulldozer, demanding that the sales or customer service staff take initiative to help.
Organization: Thing vs. Person	Person	Wants to be understood and speak to a real person who will empathize and help.

stop before treating the problem. He immediately recounted—in detail—a bad experience he had had 25 years earlier at a tailor shop. He had been getting a pair of trousers altered and had been treated very badly. As he was telling me his story, his face turned completely red: he was reliving the whole negative experience.

THE BAD EXPERIENCE REALITY

A bad experience as a customer can imprint a negative emotional state in the body and be recalled and relived in detail years later.

If you treat the customer's problem as if it were something that happens all the time, the customer is likely to believe that you are running an inefficient operation—that you know there is a problem and yet have done nothing about it. The worst example of this is when one department blames another as some sort of explanation to the customer. What are you telling your clients when you say, "I know, those guys in Operations usually mess this up"? It's apparent to the customer that the organization is dangerously out of control because *no one* is making sure the right hand is coordinated with the left.

On the other hand, if you get upset on behalf of the customer, it is as if you are stepping to their side and experiencing their frustration

with them. They will have no need to continue to be angry because you have become their advocate. An upset customer needs you to become an advocate for her, but your company needs to make sure that you are not taking the blame or accepting responsibility for something that may end up being costly.

In the next few chapters, I will expand on each of the four steps outlined in Table 7-2 in our journey toward excellence in customer service. Each step has specific behaviors and techniques. The point is to meet the customer where they are, recognize and honor their feelings as legitimate, solve the problem, make amends, and set up a better future with the customer.

TABLE 7-2 ——**Words That Change Minds Upset Customer Process and Techniques**

1. Treat the emotion first	2. Clarify what the customer wants and take action	3. Make amends	4. Nourish the relationship
Be upset on behalf of your customer.	Offer two options.	Outline how you will make amends.	Set up a positive expectation for the future.
Match their tone. Say something helpful.	Use Language of Suggestion and Language of Prevention.	Use "I" language.	Use Reassuring Tone.
Lead the tone to a lower level.		Use Special Event Tone.	Create a visual image in the client's mind of future positive experiences.

When you get upset on behalf of the customers, they believe:

- Problems are the exception, not the rule
- You are as shocked/upset as they are
- You "get it"
- You care and you are going to help
- Your organization is a caring organization
- Good people, good organization!

Many customers will express surprise when you get upset on their behalf. They are simply not used to it. Because of the typical response they get when they are upset with a product or service, they have come to believe it is necessary to fight to get their needs met.

When you go to your customer's emotional bus stop and invite them on the bus, they are much more willing to go with you than if you indicate you just want them to get over it. Match the customer's tone and key words to establish rapport. Once they know that you have heard them, you can say something helpful and they will be willing to calm down and begin to deal with the issues at hand.

This approach and these tips are designed to help you maintain and improve a positive relationship with your customers while continuing to meet your objectives. In the following chapters, you will find the skills and techniques you need to turn your upset customers into loyal customers.

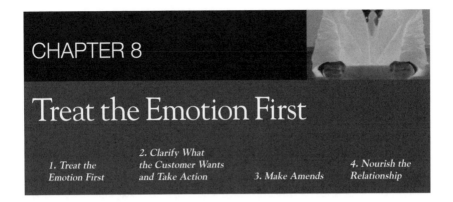

CHAPTER 8

Treat the Emotion First

1. Treat the Emotion First *2. Clarify What the Customer Wants and Take Action* *3. Make Amends* *4. Nourish the Relationship*

We were with an auto-maker client in a warning review, regarding the number of heat seat failures. The client was very Macho, in Blame mode. I needed to convince him that the problem was in the original design. Using the techniques, I listened to his tirade for 30 minutes, kept my composure and let him vent, matched his tone and got him calmed down. Then I showed him the data, explained, and answered questions. He got off the blame and asked where to go from here. I offered him two options. He considered other (non-viable) alternatives and then eliminated them himself, and we came to an agreement.

—PROGRAM MANAGER, AUTO PARTS MANUFACTURER

Most sales and customer service staff have been trained to stay calm when their customers are seething (if they have received any training at all). They propose solutions, which are often rejected out of hand. Or worse, the customer service representative becomes defensive as a reaction to feeling attacked and then refuses to be helpful. In this chapter, we will review the whys and hows of dealing with your customers' emotions. Leaders can teach these techniques to front-line staff in order to reduce escalations and increase rapport in contentious situations.

At a below-conscious level, when staff do not acknowledge and show respect for customers' emotional state, the customers are led to believe that staff are not acknowledging them as people. Remember when you were the annoyed customer who wasn't happy with a product or service? How did you feel when the representative did not truly acknowledge how you felt and the legitimacy of your complaint?

By remaining calm, the customer service representative may create a perception that the problem is just business as usual. The representative may be inadvertently sending the customer the message that her problem is an everyday occurrence—that staff are aware of the problem and that nothing is being done about it. You don't want the customer to be worried or panicked about your company's reliability just because someone handled an issue as if it were an everyday occurrence.

On the other hand, if you get upset on behalf of the customer, it is as if you are stepping into their shoes and experiencing their frustration with them. They will have no need to continue to be angry because you are on their side, working *with* them to solve the problem.

An upset customer needs you to become an advocate for her, but your company needs to make sure that you are not too quickly taking the blame or accepting responsibility for something that may end up being costly. The way to quickly get an angry customer to calm down is to get upset on her behalf, make sure she knows that you "get it," and then lead the customer to a calmer state.

I taught this approach to customer service representatives in a government employment insurance office. They often had to deal with extreme customer situations. They told me about a man who didn't receive his check and couldn't find his way through the complex bureaucracy. He became so frustrated that he turned up at their office one day, screaming at the top of his lungs and wielding a baseball bat. It is not by remaining calm and professional that you will get this man to listen to reason.

Here's how to treat the emotion first:

1. Be upset *on behalf of your customer.*
2. Match their tone.
3. Say something helpful.
4. Lead the tone to a lower level.

The employment insurance office staff have been using this technique to deal with angry people and have had very positive results.[1]

Be Upset on Behalf of the Customer

When you become upset on behalf of your customer, she will know that you *do* realize that the problem is important to her. You validate her point of view; once someone's emotions have been validated, they can begin to let them go.[2]

---

[1] Obviously, baseball-bat-wielding clients are a breed apart. These violent clients will not be part of our discussion in this chapter. However, ensure that your staff are made aware of the warning signs that anger is turning to aggression and violence. At a certain point, it is more prudent to call in the police or building security.

[2] In a 2007 survey by TD Financial Group, 84% of respondents agreed that one experience can make or break their relationship with a company, so it is important to make sure you have recognized and validated your customer's point of view.

How can you do this easily and simply? Repeat back the upset customer's key words—the ones they are probably repeating and/or shouting. Here are some examples:

CUSTOMER: This is *the third time* I've had to phone.

RESPONSE: The *third time*!?

CUSTOMER: THAT IS IT! I've *had it* with you folks. I want a refund—NOW!

RESPONSE: You've *had it*?! It was so bad you want a *refund*? What happened?

CUSTOMER: Why do I have to keep going through the same long drawn-out identification procedure? There's been no progress on resolving the problem, but you are more than willing to *waste everyone's time* by going through the same stupid process every time before we can talk about the issue that's *still not resolved*!

RESPONSE: The problem is *still not resolved*?! [Pause, wait for the customer's response.] Well, let's not *waste everyone's time* any more.

Match the Tone

It is important you find an equivalent response to your customer's tone to demonstrate that you are upset on his behalf. Remember, however, that there is a fine line between genuinely showing you are upset on the customer's behalf and just parroting his key phrases. The former can build bridges and lead to better relations, whereas the latter can serve to escalate negative emotions even faster. Table 8-1, the Words That Change Minds Customer Tone Chart, shows you how to do this by using your voice tone on the phone or in person with your client.

The chart is fairly simple to use. First, notice the tone of voice used by the customer. Is it a normal, neutral tone of voice? Is she concerned or worried about something? Is he annoyed or irritated? Table 8-1 also addresses the two major customer problem emotions: worry and its higher level, panic; and annoyance or irritation with their higher level, fury.

Secondly, use the tone of voice suited to the customer's tone. **In order to make an impact and help your customer calm down, it is important to use the following formula: match, match, match, lead.** This is a simple yet very effective process. Make at least three statements *matching* the customer's tone before moving your own tone to a lower level; you'll establish rapport through tone matching which, in turn, opens the customer to following your tone lead when you lower it. By using match, match, match,

TABLE 8-1 _____ **Words That Change Minds
Customer Tone Chart©**

Customer Tone	Your Response	Desired Response from Customer
Neutral	Warm, friendly	Warm tone of voice
Concerned, worried	Surprised, concerned, committed to finding a solution	Relieved
Annoyed, irritated	Surprised, concerned, committed to finding a solution	Calmer
Panicked	Shock, horror, dismay, committed to finding a solution	Calmer
Furious	Shock, horror, dismay, committed to finding a solution	Calmer

lead, you've opened a safe emotional path that the customer can follow. The reason this strategy is effective is not only because of the traditional "rule of three,"[3] but also because 52% of the population at work[4] is convinced by a number of examples, the most common of which is three.

When you match your customer's tone, you'll notice that she gradually loses the edge and the emotion. You are indicating your support of her by your tone, and she may no longer feel the need to argue with you. This makes it possible for her to let go of the negative emotion and to get ready to move to solutions. You will notice the customer's tone becoming calmer by your third match, opening the opportunity for you to lead the tone of the interaction to a calmer one.

Many customers express surprise when someone becomes upset on their behalf because they are simply not used to it. They've come to believe it is necessary to fight to get their needs met. Why not? That's all they've ever experienced. This common perception was the idea behind the print advertising used to promote a large bank's stress-free mortgage package. It showed a female customer holding her hands behind her back as she prepared to speak with the account manager; the customer had boxing gloves on.

Here's what some contact center staff had to say after learning this technique for dealing with angry customers:

"It was like turning a switch. The customer went from confrontational to being totally cooperative immediately.

---

[3] According to Wikipedia: "The **rule of three** is a principle in English writing that suggests that things that come in threes are inherently funnier, more satisfying, or more effective than other numbers of things."

[4] From *Words That Change Minds*, "Convincer Mode," on page 139.

I sounded shocked and she calmed down and I had a better connection with the client, who then called me by name. After that everything was easy with her.

I am listening more to people to get more in tune with their feelings to see their emotional state; then I can relate answers to them."

When you go to your customer's emotional bus stop and invite them on the bus, they are much more willing to accompany you than if you just want them to get over the emotion. Match the customer's tone and key words to get into rapport with them. Once they *see* that you have *heard* them, you can say something helpful and they will be willing to calm down and begin to deal with the issues at hand.

Here's an exchange between an angry customer and a skilled customer service representative:

CUSTOMER: I called you already three times about my broken refrigerator and *no one has gotten back to me.* In spite of the fact that I keep calling, nothing has been done and we've been *without a fridge now for over a week.* This is a very expensive new fridge and I can't believe that A. it doesn't work and B. your service stinks!

RESPONSE: *No one has gotten back to you?! No fridge for over a week?!* That's awful! [Upset on behalf of customer and tone matching.]

CUSTOMER: Yes it is. We lost over $400 worth of meat and other frozen products, and I'm not getting *any help* from anyone.

RESPONSE: $400! And you didn't get *any help!* I need to look into this right away. We need to get someone out there as soon as possible. [Saying something helpful.]

CUSTOMER: Exactly! When can someone get here? [Calmer tone.]

Response: I can find out right away, if you are okay with holding the line for a few minutes. Would that be all right?

CUSTOMER: Yes, I guess. I'm afraid of hanging up in case you don't call me back.

RESPONSE: I understand. This may take a few minutes, but I want to be sure that we solve this problem as quickly as possible.

CUSTOMER: Thank you.

The customer service representative returned a few minutes later with both an explanation and a commitment. The refrigerator was an expensive import, and the retailer had outsourced the repair back to the importer who had neglected to follow up on the call. This prompted the customer service representative to take over the file. She negotiated the time for the repair call and followed up before the service call to make sure the repair person would be on time for the appointment. The representative then followed up again with the customer to confirm the arrival time of the repair person and afterwards to make sure the work was done well.

The customer later expressed surprise at how well she had been treated. She was expecting a big fight and instead found someone who was as upset as she was and who was committed to finding a solution. **Research shows that how one treats the customer's negative emotions is key to retaining the customer.**[5]

While this kind of follow-up is certainly what the customer wanted to happen the first time and eventually led to keeping the customer, it was the representative's first responses to the upset customer that enabled the customer to participate in the solution to the problem. You will notice that the rep did not argue with the customer; she became upset on the customer's behalf, which allowed the customer to calm down quite quickly.

Shifting Someone Out of Blame Frame

Here is a technique for getting your customer out of what some have called "Blame Frame" and into thinking about what they want instead. Again, it is important not to argue with the angry customer or defend a point of view. This technique respects the customer's need to get the issues off his chest and to be heard. The purpose of this technique is to enable the customer not only to vent, but to put the emotion behind him (when he is ready, of course!) in order to move to the problem-solving phase.

Blame Frame to Outcome Frame Technique[6]

1. Listen to the problem, without interrupting. (Let the customer vent and get it off their chest.)
2. Summarize the problem using the customer's key words, but put the problem into the immediate past. In other words, try to avoid using the present tense; when you use the past, it helps the customer put the incident behind them.
   Example: *"So you've been annoyed about the delays?"*

---

[5] Marcel Zeelenberg and Rik Pieters, "A review and new findings on behavioral responses to regret and disappointment in failed services," *Science Direct: Journal of Business Research*, Vol. 57, No. 4, April, 2004, pp. 445–55. Zeelenberg and Pieters found that dissatisfaction and the specific emotions of disappointment and regret influenced customers' behavioral responses (complaining, switching, word-of-mouth, and customer inertia). **They concluded that emotions have a direct impact on behavior, over and above the effects of dissatisfaction with a product or service.**

[6] This technique has been adapted from Connirae Andreas's *Advanced Language Patterns* audio program, published by NLP Comprehensive, 1999.

3. Test to determine the customer's readiness to move to something more positive.
    Example: *"Is that right?"*

If they say yes, move to the next step (see Chapter 9, "Clarify What the Customer Wants and Take Action") to meet their needs. If they say no, keep listening until they have finished getting it out of their system. Start again at the first step, above.

Say Something Helpful

Once the customer begins to calm down you can say something helpful about solving the problem. Be careful that you are not promising too much, which might be seen as unhelpful. (For hints, see Chapter 9, "Clarify What the Customer Wants and Take Action.") A calmer person can actually hear what you have to say. You can then lead the tone to a lower level and come to grips with what needs to be done to solve the problem.

Lower the Tone

Remember match, match, match, lead? Well, now is your chance to lead.
    Example: When your customer is very angry, you could say:

> *"This **has** been **dragging on way too long** [match tone], it's got to be **really frustrating** to have to **keep calling** [match tone], when you know there **has got to be a way to fix this** [match tone], and that's what I can help you with [lead—lowered tone.]"*

Putting It Together

With the LAB Profile, you can track the shifts customers make between normal interactions and upset customer interactions. This is important because it enables you to identify the language to use and the words to avoid in order to directly impact your client's emotional state. See Table 8-2 to map out what happens when customers become upset. Front-line customer staff can easily learn these language patterns. The patterns and responses are equally effective on the phone or in person, and even during formal customer meetings.

TABLE 8-2 ———————————— **Normal vs. Upset Customer LAB Profile Patterns**

LAB Profile Patterns	Normal Interaction	Upset Customer LAB Profile Patterns	Language of Influence to Use	Words to Avoid	Desired Response
Source: Internal vs. External	**External** Willing to follow instructions	**Internal**, won't be told what to do	**Language of Suggestion**, e.g., "I suggest," "Here's what we could do"	**Directive Language**, e.g., "Do this," "Go there," "Speak to Mr. Vargas"	Consideration, then acceptance
Direction: Toward vs. Away From	**Toward** a goal or **Away From** A problem	Highly **Away From** the present problem	**Language of Prevention**, e.g., "I want to make sure that it won't happen again"	**Giving instructions** to customer without a reason	Cooperation
Reason: Options vs. Procedures	**Procedures**, will follow normal process	**Options**, wants you to break rules to fix it	**The special way**, e.g., "Usually I have to . . . but because of this problem, I'm going to . . ."	**The normal procedure**	Renewed cooperation
Organization: Person vs. Thing	**Mainly Thing**, focused on the task	**Person**, wants you to help	**The personal touch**, e.g., "I can help you, Mr. Lee"	**Thing language**, e.g., "It will have to go for repair"	A personal relationship
Stress Response: Feelings vs. Choice vs. Thinking	**Neutral Emotions**	**High Feelings**, very negative emotional state	**Match upset tone** of customer (see Table 8-1, Customer Tone Chart©)	Sounding as if the **problem is a normal** occurrence	Customer calms down

Note: as the customer moves from upset to calmer, their LAB Profile Patterns also shift back to the Normal Interaction Patterns.

"At the customer's assembly plant, their engineering staff was under a lot of pressure about the nap distortion on the cloth. They were hostile and I allowed them to vent without interruption. Then I explained the history of the material; advantages/ disadvantages and what we had been trying to do. We asked for their suggestions and they willingly conceded that we were already doing the best we can do."

—Plant Manager

Tips for Getting Upset on Behalf of the Customer

■ Raise your voice to almost match their volume; beware of sounding ironic or mocking, or angry *at* the customer

■ Make an exclamation of surprise and distress:

For example, *"What!"* or *"You're kidding!"*

■ Treat this problem like the emergency it is for the customer

■ Repeat the customer's key words (words repeated or stressed) back to them

■ Make sure you fully understand the customer's situation by stating back exactly what you understood.

For example, "I just want to be completely sure I've got it. You brought your computer in **three weeks ago** and you keep calling and **it's still not ready?**"

> *"I just had the most incredible experience yesterday with someone that could have been a disaster but turned out pretty positively, because I employed some of the skills you taught us, specifically matching and reading their reaction."*
> —GENERAL MANAGER, APPLIED SOLUTIONS,
> FROM A FINANCIAL GROUP

Sales and customer service people who help others solve problems have far less stress than those who feel constantly battered by angry, unreasonable customers. As Miller and Dell Smith write:[7]

> *"Chronic stress is the result of unrelenting demands and pressures for seemingly interminable periods of time. This is the grinding stress that wears people away day after day, year after year and it wreaks havoc through long-term attrition."*

When employees are subjected to a constant barrage of stressful communications, they can suffer emotional distress themselves in some combination of anger or irritability, anxiety, and depression—the three stress emotions.

Imagine what a difference it would make to sales and customer service employees, for their morale and in their performance, when they view their role as being an advocate on behalf of the customers.

---

[7] Lyle H. Miller, Ph.D., and Alma Dell Smith, Ph.D., "The Stress Solution," in *The Different Kinds of Stress*, American Psychological Association, 2004.

"A customer was rejecting parts because of the trimming, blaming us and getting very angry. I managed to shift the meeting to a more solution focus very quickly and we discussed standards. They rewrote the specs and we agreed. They admitted it was originally their issue. We came up with better criteria and the number of parts returned was not affected. And I felt like I had really helped solve a critical problem, both for them and for us."
—PROGRAM MANAGER

Once you have calmed the upset customer down, you can then clarify what they want and need. The following case illustrates how an entire call center dealt with what could have been a public relations disaster.

Perfect Storm Success Story in Halton Region
CASE STUDY

On April 7, 2008, the regional municipality of Halton in Ontario, Canada introduced a new waste management system to 135,000 households. Residents would now put most of their waste into either a recycle bin (newspapers, cans, cardboard, etc.) or a GreenCart for organic matter (food scraps) to be composted. Recycling and Green-Cart materials would be collected every week and garbage only once every two weeks. Prior to this program, garbage was collected every week and recycling material every two weeks, so it was a significant behavior change for residents.

The municipality's communication division and customer call center, known as "Access Halton," were ready. Advertisements appeared in all the newspapers and brochures were sent to households, along with calendars showing exactly what would be collected on which dates. As one can imagine with the introduction of such a large new program, some logistical issues arose with the rollout of the program.

A flood of calls came into the call center. While Access Halton normally answers approximately 5,300 waste management calls per month, they answered 29,379 waste management calls during the first month of the new program. The call center had increased staff to get ready for the rollout, but it was difficult for them to obtain specific and immediate information about what was being done to remedy some of the issues, because the waste management department was also stretched in making sure the problems were being solved and the program was being implemented and delivered effectively.

These factors added up to the perfect storm for call center staff.

Access Halton staff listed the types of calls they received:

1. People primarily requesting information on what waste went into which bin. 7,219 (24%) of calls were general waste-related questions. For example, how to place materials curbside for GreenCart, bulk garbage and recycling, and what went into the GreenCart.

2.   Inquiries and complaints regarding when GreenCart would be delivered. Not all residents received a GreenCart prior to launch of the program—5,807 (19%) of calls were related to GreenCart delivery. Some examples of these calls were: "When is the GreenCart going to arrive?" "Can I get a second one?" "How come everyone else received their GreenCart and I didn't?"

3.   People refusing to follow the new system.

4.   People wanting weekly garbage collection as before.

5.   Questions regarding how much the new waste management program cost.

6.   Forty ways the region could have handled the rollout better.

7.   Criticisms that the region hadn't put any planning into the program.

8.   Complaints regarding late pickup of waste and recyclables during the first week.

9.   People enthusiastic about the new program but frustrated and confused about implementation issues.

The call center had very experienced staff who had participated in my training on handling upset customers. I asked them how they handled the fury. They said it was very important to let the customer vent without interrupting. When they occasionally interrupted, they found it made people angrier than they already were. Once they had heard the customers out and expressed how much they understood their frustration, they explained the purpose of the program and acknowledged some of the issues in the rollout that residents were facing. They apologized when there were logistical problems. And for those who refused to participate in the program, they invited them to try it out for two weeks and to let them know what they thought of it.

"It was amazing how quickly some residents became upset about their garbage not being collected on time," commented Access Halton manager Ron MacMaster. "However, during all that time not one complaint was received about our call center staff."

The call center staff had the additional difficulty of not always having the most up-to-date information to relay to residents. They apologized when necessary and had the full and complete support of their director of community relations, Carleen Carroll, the chief administrative officer, Pat Moyle, and the Halton region chair, Gary Carr, who each came into the call center several times to offer their appreciation and encouragement. While it was anticipated that there would be difficulties with the start-up, it was very encouraging to see the entire organization pull together to problem-solve and quickly resolve the issues for Halton residents.

When I went to see them shortly after the rollout, I asked for some tricks of the trade that other call center professionals in the same situation might use. They responded with the following list:

1.   Apologize, acknowledge frustration, and give the best information available.

2.   Don't take it personally, be mature, and recognize they are not upset at you, even if some people say mean things.

3.   If someone yells with a very loud voice, turning down the volume on the headset helps to stay calm inside.

4. Establish boundaries if needed, if people become overly abusive.
5. Create good communication with other involved departments, so that you can have the most up-to-date information.
6. Vent to co-workers when you get frustrated, but keep your sense of humor.
7. Become the duck metaphor ("your feet doing all the paddling underneath while above the surface there is calm and smooth sailing").
8. Be familiar with all the resources of the region; many answers are in there.
9. Remember that the callers know nothing about the region and the programs, and that one role of the call center is to inform and educate.

I asked them about what they learned personally and professionally from having weathered the perfect call center storm. Here are some of their answers:

"I learned a lot about people. What's important to one person may not be important to you, but they want you to empathize. They want you to care."

"I got a thicker skin and learned not to take things so personally."

"As a team, I feel we can handle everything. We have loyalty and commitment and we did it together."

"We really got to know each other—we really grounded each other."

"It increased my confidence."

"It made me a better complainer—I try not to shoot the messenger."

"I understood that people will get angry over the silliest things, but I still have to deal with them."

"I thought to myself that if this is the worst thing you have to deal with, then things aren't so bad."

It's no surprise that the Halton Region call center earned the coveted Service Quality Management Highest Customer Satisfaction rating for government in 2006.

This chapter described the critical first step in dealing with an upset customer. The following chapters outline how to ensure you meet all their needs and set up a positive relationship for the future.

CHAPTER 9

The Two-Solution Solution

1. Treat the Emotion First	2. Clarify What the Customer Wants and Take Action	3. Make Amends	4. Nourish the Relationship

Once you have calmed your upset customer by becoming an advocate on his behalf, he needs to know the next step. Since he was unhappy with what happened, it is important to clarify what he needs now if you want to retain his respect and loyalty and prevent him from looking for a new supplier.

Taking the time to clarify what your customer wants allows you to regain credibility in the customer's eyes, so make sure you can provide something he or she wants. It also gives your customer a choice. When you use this strategy, you begin to rebuild the trust that was lost with the customer. Use this technique whenever you are ready to shift attention to solutions. There are a number of ways of finding out what your customer will be satisfied with:

1. Offer two options, then summarize.
2. The Bad News Formula.
3. The "While I can't . . . , I can . . ." Formula.
4. "I wish I could give you everything you want."

We'll discuss each step in detail below.

Offer Two Options

Instead of asking the customer what she wants, make a couple of proposals and ask if one would meet her needs. This is the "Two-Solution Solution." This strategy will enable you to uncover what the customer wants or needs, given all that has happened. For many people, it is easier to figure out what you want when someone suggests something, rather than having to think about it in a vacuum. The fact that the problem occurred may have created a different need. Or perhaps what your customer originally wanted may not be feasible.

To keep the customer focused on moving forward and motivated by what you say, you can match the major LAB Profile Patterns of the upset customer when proposing something; Table 9-1 below lays it all out for you.

TABLE 9-1 — **LAB Profile Patterns and Language of Influence for Upset Customers**

LAB Profile Patterns	Upset Customer LAB Profile Patterns	Language of Influence
Source: Internal vs. External	**Internal**	Use the Language of Suggestion when making proposals for them to consider, rather than Command Language.
Reason: Options vs. Procedures	**Options**	Propose two solutions and use the words "options" or "choices."
Direction: Toward vs. Away From	**Away From**	Talk about what your suggestions will prevent or how to move away from the problem.

When you offer two options to your customer, it is important to say what the options will *prevent* (Away From language). Make sure you are using the Language of Suggestion to leave the choice up to your customer. This way, you avoid being perceived as overly directive.

Example:

Customer Service Representative	Influencing Language
"So that we don't waste any more of your time, I suggest	Away From—Prevention Internal—Language of Suggestion
Two options: that either we credit your account right away or apply this against your next purchase.	Options—Choices, either/or
What do you think?"	Internal—Invitation to decide

As you can see from the above, *"So that we don't waste any more of your time"* is in Away From, Prevention Language, which matches the customer's desire to avoid further problems. *"I suggest"* is the Language of Suggestion, which appeals to people who want to make their own decisions. Finally, *"What do you think?"* invites the customer to decide for herself, which keeps to her Internal motivation trigger. Note that Options language is built right into the sentence: the customer service representative proposes two options, as well as using *"either/or."*

It is easier for a customer to decide what is important to them when you make a suggestion. They will think about your suggestions, and you can sort out what is important to them by really paying attention to their reaction and by listening to their response. If you were to simply ask a customer, "What would you like us to do now?" you might risk throwing them back into a negative, accusatory mindset, especially if they expect you to be the expert who knows what needs to be done. It is even worse if the customer service representative doesn't make any suggestions at all and waits for the customer to take the initiative.

Here's the formula for the Two-Solution Solution:

> Since we want to prevent [x problem] from occurring again,
> I'd like to suggest two options for you to consider; either [option 1]
> or [option 2]. What do you think?

My mobile phone provider has a long way to go in understanding how to recover from having angered their customers. I had canceled two of four business phone contracts because the plans were costing too much, and I managed, with much persistence and some aggression (I admit) on my part, to get the supervisor's supervisor to agree to reduce the penalty from $400 to $200. I tried to get him to eliminate the penalty altogether, but he not only refused, he threatened to remove the deal from the table—a deal to which he had already agreed—if I didn't take it immediately. I reluctantly agreed, having decided that it would be impossible to get any more from them.

Then, on my next bill, as plain as day, was the full $400 penalty! What about all the time I had spent getting it reduced? One more phone call resulted in them removing the extra $200, but I was still very annoyed.

Shortly after that, I received a call from their telemarketing department. The telemarketer began by acknowledging that I had paid a penalty for canceling two phones and immediately went on to talk about a service that I could get for free for a few months in compensation. I stopped her procedure to let her know that I was still very annoyed with the company about having to pay the penalty. She said: "I know, but what I want to talk to you about is . . ." and on she continued, telling me about this new service. I couldn't let this pass. "Look," I said, "I think this is just a con to get me to spend more money, and I would really rather have the $200 penalty credited to my bill." "Are you accusing me of conning you?" she asked, raising her voice. The conversation went downhill from there.

Do you think they were recording this conversation to improve customer service? Have I been called since? No. Perhaps they put me in their difficult customer category.

She could have prevented the whole debacle by simply acknowledging how frustrating it was to have to pay a penalty when I first said I was upset. She could have made a couple of little "tut, tut" noises and waited for me to get it off my chest. Then she could have phrased her offer by linking it to my dissatisfaction.

Here's how she could have handled my anger and frustration:

> "That's why I'm calling you. We know you were upset with what happened, and we didn't want you to be unhappy, so we have a couple of things we can do for you that we hope you will consider."

Clearly the company was attempting to regain my goodwill, but had no real idea how to do it.

But you won't be making that mistake once you know the two-solution solution! Once you've offered the customer two choices you need to get him to decide. If you have offered x and y, he may just accept one of those options, in which case you can summarize what you have just agreed to with the customer.

The Bad News Formula[1]

Alternatively, your customer may not want x or y: she may want z. If you are authorized to agree to z, you have the solution. If you cannot give her z, you will need to handle this part of the conversation to keep the customer on your side. This is where the Bad News Formula comes in handy to get your message across without re-angering the client.

My definition of bad news is "anything a person does not want to hear." In a customer service context, not getting what he or she wants is bad news for the customer. The Bad News Formula relies on the "Principle of Recency"[2]: that is, the last thing a person hears is what sticks with them. This formula is also built upon the general perception that any statement followed by the word "but" is diminished. What comes after the "but"

---

[1] The Bad News Formula is quoted from two Neuro-linguistic Programming trainers, Veli-Matti Toivonen and Tim Murphey, on the impact of using the words "but" and "and."

[2] From Wikipedia: The principle of **recency** states that things most recently learned are best remembered.

leaves a stronger impression. Statements on either side of the word "and" are perceived by most people to have equal strength.

Here's how it goes:

First, make sure you have established a good level of rapport with your customer. Then, use the following formula in explaining the options available:

Example:

> I can't give you a refund, BUT I can give you a discount on
> your next purchase AND you can make this purchase at any time
> AND apply it to any item you want from our catalog.

It is important to have already established a good level of rapport with the customer before using the Bad News Formula, or the bad news part will be perceived as too abrupt.

The "While I Can't" Formula

Here's an alternative to the Bad News Formula: The While I Can't Formula.

> While I can't do x, I CAN do y.

> While I can't give you a refund, I CAN give you a discount on your
> next purchase.

To use these strategies effectively, each sales or service staff member needs to know what they are allowed to offer to the customer, as well as the process for expressing these offers. As illustrated by my mobile phone fiasco, only having an offer to make up for a problem is insufficient to mollify a customer on the edge. Customer service representatives need to have the authority to do something meaningful for the customer.

Lee Valley Garden Tools customer service representatives have permission to refund a customer up to the total of what they have paid, without asking for a supervisor's permission. It's up to the customer service representative to decide what's fair.

The "I Wish I Could Give You Everything" Formula

What if your client insists on getting their way? Here is where you need to express sadness at not being able to do everything they want. This technique comes from Adele Faber and Elaine Mazlish's excellent parenting book *How to Talk So Kids Will Listen and Listen So Kids Will Talk*.[3] They suggest that you say, "Gee, I wish I could give you everything you want." Using this phrase in a customer service environment lets the client know that you *are* on her side and that you wish you could do what she wants. Make sure you are ready with a couple of alternatives to suggest after that, or let the customer know that you will get back to her with some solutions.

When you have several tools at your disposal to clarify what your customer wants, it makes meeting most customers' needs easier, even when they are very insistent. You can even use these techniques one after another to solve the issue on first contact instead of having the customer escalate to management.

Here is an example of how to clarify what the customer wants:

SERVICE REPRESENTATIVE: Here's what I suggest [Internal—Language of Suggestion] to make sure you don't have to wait any longer for a service call [Away From—Prevention Language]; either I can book the appointment for you right now while you hold for a couple of minutes, or I can get the service department to call you directly in the next few minutes [two options] to book the appointment. Which would you prefer?"

CUSTOMER: What I really want is some compensation for all the trouble I've been through. I think you owe me that.

SERVICE REPRESENTATIVE: I'm sorry about what happened to you. It shouldn't have happened. [pause] I can't give you compensation, BUT I can make sure this situation gets resolved right away AND I will stay on the line to make sure you get the appointment right away AND I will follow up with you after the appointment to make sure it went well. [Bad News Formula]

CUSTOMER: That sounds okay. I can live with that. But what about throwing in the new hardware for free?

SERVICE REPRESENTATIVE: Hmmm, while I can't do that, I can make sure that if there are any problems in the basic hardware you already have, it gets replaced right away at no cost. Would that be all right? [While I Can't Formula]

CUSTOMER: Okay.

---

[3] *How to Talk So Kids Will Listen & Listen So Kids Will Talk* by Adele Faber and Elaine Mazlish, Collins Living, 1999.

SERVICE REPRESENTATIVE: So, I will make sure that you get the service call appointment right away and follow up with you afterward and make sure that if there are any problems in the basic hardware, they are fixed [summary]. Thanks for letting me know about the problem. I will also check with our systems people to make sure the appointment-setting procedure is working to avoid this sort of thing in the future.

Special Case: Security Breaches and Identity Theft

Identity theft has been an issue for clients of financial institutions and other sectors, including government, as government departments have outsourced data management. It is not uncommon to receive correspondence from your financial institution notifying you of security breaches at one of their data centers where financial information is stored.

Credit card customers know they are relatively safe from illegal use of their cards, because credit card companies have a well-established procedure for enabling customers to report stolen or misused cards and be exonerated from paying for most illegal uses of the cards. On the other hand, protection from identity theft or security breaches is far from the established norm. There are still occasional reports of people having to go through expensive court battles to regain title to their own houses.

As governments and health management organizations have been creating processes for managing health information online, as well as tax, passport, and birth certificate information, citizens have been wondering whether they can trust the system. It took time for people to trust online purchase systems, and it wasn't until security systems and procedures for fixing security breaches were in place that customers felt more at ease with this buying channel.

Procedure, Not Options

When there is a security breach and you are solving the problem for your business or consumer customer, it is important that you have one clear procedure that will fix the problem. Instead of providing the customer with a couple of options, as mentioned above, it is important that you only provide one procedure. If you suggest options in this situation, the customer may believe that you don't know the right way to solve the problem and may begin to feel even more worried or upset.

I suggest that you use very Procedural Language. For example:

The first step is . . . the second step is . . . and the last step is . . .

followed by Away From—Prevention Language:

> That way you won't have the hassle of coming in here.

or

> So the problem will be fixed as soon as possible and you won't
> have to worry about it.

You can be more directive about this because you need to demonstrate that you are certain about what to do next. Of course, this presupposes that your organization has already developed a procedure for dealing with security breaches that will protect your customers.

In this chapter, we covered the second crucial step for recovering the goodwill of the customer: clarifying what they want. As illustrated, it is important to use the correct Influencing Language to make sure they focus on the positive. The next step is to make amends to begin to repair the relationship. I'll cover that topic in the next chapter, and after that we'll examine how to ensure that your customers are looking forward to doing business again and again with your organization in the future.

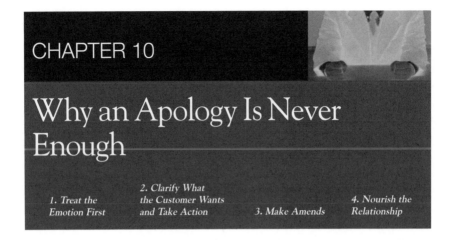

CHAPTER 10

Why an Apology Is Never Enough

1. Treat the Emotion First	2. Clarify What the Customer Wants and Take Action	3. Make Amends	4. Nourish the Relationship

When your customer feels he has been wronged, it is not enough to fix the problem and apologize—not if your real goal is to ensure that he will *want* to continue to do business with you.

Dictionary.com defines "make amends" as "to compensate, as for an injury, loss, or insult." This is exactly the principle to apply as part of the Words That Change Minds Upset Customer Process. Your goal is to let the customer know on an emotional level that you are serious about doing what it takes to keep him happy (not just to keep him as a customer, but to keep him happy). It is exactly the same principle your parents may have taught you when, as a child, you hurt someone's feelings or did something bad and you were told that you had to "make it up to them."

As you know, when someone has wronged you, you may have a feeling that they *owe* you something. This feeling arises because basically the relationship has become unbalanced, and will stay so until balance is restored. In the same vein, customers who feel they were wronged in some way want it put right.

This step is crucial when your organization has created the problem for the customer. However, if you have done nothing wrong, there is no absolute need to make amends but making amends will ensure that the customer *wants* to continue doing business with you.

The Make Amends Policy

When your organization has a Make Amends policy in place, your front-line sales and customer service staff can implement it whether they are seeing the client in person, speaking to the client from a contact center, or replying to an electronic communication. Have a scale that the staff can use to decide for themselves how to compensate a client. If front-line staff can decide for themselves about how to make customers happy, you'll have fewer escalations to management and more resolutions to customer issues within one contact: everyone wins.

In our company, for example, in the rare case where someone has ordered products and they haven't arrived, not only will we reship, we will often pay for expedited shipping to make amends for not having the books as soon as our customer needed them.

For a Make Amends system to work, front-line staff members need to have clear guidelines and permission to use their own judgment. The guidelines need to outline what the Make Amends policy is designed to accomplish. In other words, it needs to be clear that the desired result is to ensure the customer gets to feel that you have "made up" for the inconvenience that they experienced.

Table 10-1 is a replica of the Make Amends policy chart we use in our products business. It can be adapted to your own product or service offerings.

TABLE 10-1 ————————————————————————— **Make Amends Policy**

Goal: After having dealt with any negative emotions that the customer might have felt, clarified what the customer wants, and found an acceptable solution, the goal is to make sure the customer feels that you have "made it up to him or her" at a reasonable cost.

Problem	$ Value of Problem	Customer Negative Emotion Rating (Customer Stress Level)	Make Amends Options (Examples)	Sample Script— Using Special Event Tone	Desired Customer Response
Products didn't arrive on time	Price of products: <$50	Low	Reship by express	"Because of this problem, I'd like to make it up to you by . . ."	Expresses satisfaction
Defective or damaged products	$100–200	Low	Upgrade shipping at no cost to customer	"Since this has been stressful for you, I'd like to . . ."	Expresses appreciation
	$200–500	Medium	Send a product of similar value for free	"Since this has been stressful for you, I'd like to . . ."	Expresses appreciation
	>$500	High	Upgrade shipping and give product of similar value	"I'm so sorry that [this problem] occurred and I'd really like to make it up to you . . ."	Expresses gratitude

"I" Language

When front-line sales and customer service staff have the power to make amends when things go wrong, it is easy for them to speak on their own behalf, saying, for example, "Here's what I'd like to do for you to make up for the inconvenience."

If the customer service person says, "On behalf of the bank, we would like to do this for you to make up for the inconvenience," it can leave the impression that the staff member has no ability to make decisions or be of any real help should it be needed. It can sound as if they are just parroting the usual company policy. Instead, use "I" to communicate to the customer that they are speaking to the person who has the power to solve the problem and take care of them. This use of "I" will further reduce the number of escalated calls to management. An alternative that you could use is "The bank has authorized me to offer you . . ." though I suspect this will not be perceived as being as personal as "I" language.

The goal here is to have the customer conclude, based on their experience, that your organization has good people who care and therefore, your organization is a good organization.

Make It Personal: The Special Event Tone

Each time the customer comes into your environment, in person, on the phone, or online, it is a special event for him. Communicating with customers is what professional sales and customer service staff do all day long, but for customers, it is *not* part of their routine to have to deal with problems in products or services.

Your voice tone needs to reflect that special communication, particularly since you want the customer to know that what you are doing is something out of the ordinary when you are making amends.

I call this voice tone the "Special Event Tone." It is the tone you use when you want to tell someone something out of the ordinary. It is almost like when you have a secret to tell someone: your voice is a little breathier, with a bit of a whisper. If this weren't a book, I'd demonstrate it for you! This tone tells people to pay particular attention to what you're saying, because it isn't an everyday thing. You are doing something special to make up for the customer's inconvenience.

Here are some examples:

> Listen, Mr. Jonas, because the repair took too long, I'd like to give you one month free service.

I'm glad we cleared up the problem, Simone, but since it shouldn't have happened at all, I'd like to make it up to you and credit your account with $10 that you can use against your next order.

I really appreciate your perseverance while we fixed the problem, Mr. Patel, so I'd like to say thanks by giving you a free rental.

Notice that the apology or problem statement is said first and the offer last. Leave the best impression for last while the bad stuff (talking about the problem) is covered at the beginning. If you say, "I'd like to credit your account with $10 that you can use against your next purchase, because the problem shouldn't have happened," it reminds your customer of the problem you caused them, rather than what you are prepared to do to make it up to them.

LAB Profile Patterns of Making Amends

In the Words That Change Minds Upset Customer Process, the first two steps (treat the emotion first; clarify what the customer wants and take action) help you calm the customer and determine what is important for him. If you have done this well, the customer will move from the Upset Customer Profile to a calmer state and will more readily accept the third step of making amends. Tables 10-2 and 10-3 illustrate the changes the customer will go through and exhibit as she calms down.

TABLE 10-2

Upset Customer Profile: Expectations and Behaviors

LAB Profile Category	Upset Customer LAB Profile Patterns	Expectations and Behaviors
Source: Internal vs. External	**Internal**	Decides for themselves, hard to influence.
Direction: Toward vs. Away From	**Away From**	Notices what is wrong with what the other said or what won't work.
Stress Response: Feelings vs. Choice vs. Thinking	**Feelings**	Stuck in a highly negative emotional state.
Reason: Options vs. Procedures	**Options**	Wants alternatives and willing to break rules to get what they want. Won't follow the normal procedure.
Level: Proactive vs. Reactive	**Proactive** expectations that the rep will take the initiative	Likely to be a bulldozer, expecting the sales or customer service staff to take the initiative to help.
Organization: Person vs. Thing	**Person**	Wants to be understood and speak to a real person who will empathize and help.

TABLE 10-3 ————— **Upset Customer Becoming Calm Profile:**
Expectations and Behaviors

LAB Profile Patterns	LAB Profile: Customer Becoming Calm	Expectations and Behaviors
Level: Proactive vs. Reactive	Slightly **Reactive**	Will listen and respond to what you say.
Source: Internal vs. External	Mainly **Internal**	Still decides for self if she is okay with what you are proposing, but will listen.
Stress Response: Feelings vs. Choice vs. Thinking	Moving toward **Choice**	Exits the highly emotional Feelings state and chooses to become calmer.

Since the upset customer is *in the process* of changing her emotional state to become calmer, this less emotionally upset state can be very temporary. This can present a problem: almost any step in the wrong direction can set the customer off again. But by making amends, you will firm up the calmer state—and the relationship—by making sure the customer feels that you have followed through on correcting the problem. This perception of good service is vital to ensuring loyalty for the majority of customers.[1]

Overall, the most important element in this step of the Words That Change Minds Upset Customer Process is to have the customer feel you have put the interaction back in balance by offering something special for what has happened. This reaffirms the relationship the customer has with your sales and customer service front-line staff and lets the customer know that your organization is a good one with which to do business.

The final step of the Words That Change Minds Upset Customer Process is to nourish the relationship for the future, which we'll examine next.

---

[1] An Ipsos-Reid survey for TD Financial Services in 2007 indicated that 74% of customers prefer receiving good service over receiving gifts or having a donation made to a charity. http://www. newswire.ca/en/releases/archive/May2007/09/c6636.

CHAPTER 11

Create a Positive Image in Your Customer's Mind

	2. Clarify What		
1. Treat the	*the Customer Wants*		*4. Nourish the*
Emotion First	*and Take Action*	*3. Make Amends*	*Relationship*

Is it enough to calm down your angry customer, clarify what she wants, make sure you can deliver it, and make amends? Is there any purpose to keeping a customer on the phone longer, when everyone has more than enough to do? Aren't you also wasting the customer's time?

If you haven't set the client up with what he can expect in the future, he may not be any easier to deal with the next time he interacts with your company (if he does). It is essential to ensure that he is indeed motivated to continue doing business with you.

Nourishing the relationship is simply the natural end to the process of dealing with an upset customer. The crisis has been recognized. The wounds have been healed. Solutions have been found. You have made amends to the injured party. Each of these steps enabled you to handle the present emotional and product or service issues for the customer. Now it's time to set up the future.

The purpose of the Nourishing the Relationship step is to get the customer to imagine the positive relationship, services, or products they will receive in the future; it sets up a positive expectation. However, this might be a dangerous thing to do if your organization cannot deliver on these expectations, because, as we all know from personal experience, letdowns can be worse than having no expectations at all. It is important that all staff be versed in how to go about this step so that false expectations aren't created.

This step needs to be done in informal language, not as the scripted statement often used by contact center staff. You are speaking directly to a person who is your customer.

First, check if there is anything else that the customer needs from you at the moment. Secondly, reassure the customer that she can count on you to help her out with anything she needs in the future. If appropriate, give her your extension number or mention that your colleagues can also be counted on to make sure her needs get dealt with promptly.

Example:

I want to tell you that you can call anyone here; they're all great to deal with.

Tips

- End on a positive note for the future:

Is there anything else I can help you with today?
You know, you can call us any time to help with anything that comes up.

- Use person-to-person language—informal, personable. Make sure it doesn't sound like you are reading a script.
- Make it visual—be very descriptive so the customer can see in her mind's eye the next positive experience she will have with you. When she has the image in her mind, it becomes more real and, as a result, more likely to happen.

Examples:

The next time, when you pick up the phone and dial us, everyone here will be happy to make sure we can help you.

The next time you walk into our store, you can just ask anyone— we're all happy to help you.

The Problem with Formality

Many contact center staff have been inadvertently trained to be much too formal and remote at key moments in the conversation with the customer. It has frequently been my experience that, after having had a reasonable conversation with a real person who has conducted some transaction for me or solved a problem, suddenly at the end of the conversation they say something like "Thank you for doing business with us today, Ms. Rose Charvet."

I understand that **many are still evaluated on whether or not they have used the customer's name or finished the transaction with the customer's name, but this forces them to ruin the relationship they have worked so hard to create with the customer.** People simply do not want to be treated as a filled-in blank in the script.

Formality has a place in customer communications, but it is more important to establish the kind of relationship the *customer* wants to have with your organization. Many customers want to know that they are dealing with a real person who cares and can help them when a problem has occurred.

I have coached marketing departments in financial institutions and software companies on how to write letters to their customers. The key is having a real person speaking to a real customer with easy ways for the customer to get back into contact with the person. Anonymous letters or even overly formal letters with no means of getting back in touch with the person who wrote the letter do nothing to improve customer loyalty.

I had an extended correspondence by snail mail with a federal government department employee about an urgent request I had. This person would wait several weeks after I couriered her with the answers to one set of questions, then mail a response with a *new* set of questions instead of an answer to my request. I tried in vain to find a way to speed up the process; there was no way to contact her except by mail. Eventually I managed—through a third party—to reach her supervisor, who apologized to me and gave me a phone number and an immediate positive response to my request.

I compare that experience with another one where I received a letter from someone at City Hall that I didn't completely understand. The author of the letter included her e-mail address and phone number, so it was very easy to contact her and obtain the information I needed.

In-Person Sales and Service Applications

When you are interacting with your customer in person and you have resolved an issue or problem for them and have made amends, it is mainly in the nonverbal element that you can nourish the relationship for the next time.

First, check that everything has been resolved satisfactorily:

> So, you're okay with what we've set up for you now, Gene?

Then, use the Reassuring Tone, which is a warm, personable tone of voice, and an open arm gesture to let them know that you can be counted on any time in the future.

> Any time you need something, just let me know. If I'm not here, all of my colleagues would be happy to help you.

LAB Profile Patterns for Nourishing the Relationship

The LAB Profile Patterns essential in this step are the Away From a Problem, Toward a Goal Pattern, and the Person Pattern. At this stage of the communication, you want to ensure a positive outcome for future dealings with the customer, as well as heal and move away from the mistrust that may have resulted from the triggering incident.

Example:

> I'm so happy that we solved the problem so that it *won't happen again* [Away From] and I want you to know that *anyone here can help you* [Toward] anytime you need something. [Pause.] Is there anything else that you need from me right now [person's first name if appropriate]?

The use of the customer's name (either their first name or Mr./Ms./ etc.) is appropriate if it flows naturally. The tone of voice for nourishing the relationship needs to be warm and reassuring.

In this last step, think about the emotional state you want your customer to be in when he or she is leaving your establishment or about to hang up the phone. If you are clear that you want them to believe in and feel confident with you because you have proven your worth to them, you are likely to exhibit the behaviors that will lead to this and will probably say the right things. You want to link this feeling with future contacts so that you have set up the customer to have a positive experience the next time.

This wraps up the four-step Words That Change Minds Upset Customer Process, designed to ensure that your front line can recover from a sales or service failure and bring back your customer's goodwill. It is important that staff who deal directly with customers—in either sales or service—are trained in both the Upset Customer Process and the Customer Transaction Process, so they are ready for anything. It is also critical to give them the ability to compensate clients to a certain level and meet their needs. This will reduce the number of escalations and the time it takes to resolve customer issues. In the next section, we will cover communication strategies, how to hire for the best customer experience, and how to make sure that your brand is alive through your whole organization. The Irish Continental Group case study in Chapter 13 will give you an A to Z example of how to do this, using the LAB Profile as an essential tool. The last section of this book takes on other critical persuasion challenges leaders face.

PART 5

Advanced Influencing Strategies for Transforming Communication and Behavior

CHAPTER 12

The Rules Have Changed: Mass Communication

The rules have changed. In the multi-channel universe where we live, customer communication needs to reflect a profound understanding of how customers feel, think, and behave at each point of contact. **People tend to behave differently when they are on the phone, in an in-person environment, sending an e-mail, or ordering products online.** While your marketing needs to reflect your company's identity and values through each of these channels, it is also important to research how your customers' emotions, thoughts, and behaviors change as they interact with you in these different ways.

In this chapter we will explore how to use the LAB Profile in market research to uncover the essential Patterns that motivate and entice your customers, as well as how to conduct campaigns and manage your customers' experience throughout their dealings with your organization. There are many ways to use this tool to improve what you are already doing.

Organizations have been conducting psychological analyses of their customers for many years in order to increase their impact and influence, particularly in mass marketing and election campaigns. Even though sophisticated instruments are available, I suspect that much of what mass audiences are thinking and feeling can still be very difficult to track. The vice president of marketing in a large U.S. credit card company approached me because her company wanted to improve its results in direct marketing campaigns. She told me that they had spent years tweaking sales letters, and even though staff had significant experience and success in their campaigns and were measuring the results, the department was still largely ignorant about what exactly made their letters successful. They also did not know why different formats obtained different results. The LAB Profile can provide some important clues to solve these dilemmas if used rigorously.

The Context Is King

Experience using the LAB Profile for understanding and influencing customer behavior has shown over and over that the customer's Patterns will shift depending upon the Context, or situation in which they find themselves. **People usually identify the Context they are in by telling you where, when, and with whom, as well as by the verbs they choose.**
Consider these two statements:

When we are presently identifying the specifications for new business management software.

versus

Our senior team is meeting to make the final choice of software supplier.

These two statements come from two different phases in the buying cycle, and therefore they are different Contexts for the customer; as a result, the LAB Profile Patterns may not be the same for each situation. Customers may have one set of Patterns when they are gathering information about what they need for a product or service (specifications) and a different set of Patterns when they are actually making a buying decision.

For example, when a team is thinking about what they need in a new software package, they may have the following Patterns: Reactive (thinking, not doing), Options (considering many possibilities), Internal (creating their own Criteria), and Sameness with Exception (they want something better, not completely different from what they had before). When they are choosing the final supplier, the Patterns may be as follows: Mainly Proactive (making the decision), Internal (evaluating based on what is important to them), and Procedures (following a clear decision-making process).

Similarly, when customers are going through their normal transactions, they are usually running a different combination of LAB Profile Patterns than during problem transactions.

A colleague of mine decoded the LAB Profile Patterns for customers in the different lines of business for a financial institution. She determined that for each line of business, different combinations of LAB Profile Patterns were at play for customers. Her role, taking into account these Patterns as well as other information, was to determine the overall branding for the whole financial institution, as well as to identify the keys for each line of business separately: i.e., high value investing, transactional banking, and insurance (the different kinds of insurance).

From her research, key behaviors were identified that customer representatives and sales staff needed to have for each of the businesses to match the customers' needs and LAB Profile Patterns. We then trained team leaders and contact center staff in some of the businesses so they could provide the customers with what they needed. We also trained the contact center staff in the Words That Change Minds Upset Customer Process, as this was determined to be important for them. While I cannot reveal actual research findings, you can imagine that if she found that customers for one line of business were mainly Internal during normal transactions, then we trained the call center staff to use Internal Influencing Language, by making suggestions instead of using Command Language, etc.

Several years ago, a friend of mine asked me to help her with her election campaign. After many years of serving on the local school board, she had decided to run for municipal council. At the time she ran for election, many local municipalities had been swiftly merged into one municipal unit by the new provincial government. Many other changes had taken place that affected the daily lives of residents: the province had downloaded new fiscal and program responsibilities to the municipal level, the number of elected officials had changed, and it had become unclear which level of government was responsible for which functions.

In order to prepare for her campaign, I asked her to gather important information regarding the local electorate. All of her canvassers were directed to ask residents the following question:

What is important to you at the moment you are deciding who to vote for, for municipal council?

This question is very Context-specific. **We wanted to know all the Criteria (the words, phrases, and images that act as a person's labels for what they want or think is important or right in a given context) and LAB Profile Patterns that would come into play at the moment people were making their voting decision.** We didn't know where or when they would be making the decision, so we needed to be vague about that, but we were able to pinpoint the exact Context we wanted to study. Had we not understood the importance of Context, we might have made the mistake of simply asking, "What is important to you in a municipal councilor?" **This question would have been too general for the purpose of understanding the prime motivators at the moment of decision.**

Since we had the opportunity to ask voters only one question at that time, we picked the LAB Profile Criteria question. Typically, when people answer the question "What do you want?" or "What is important to you about . . .?" embedded in their answer are not only their Criteria, but phrases indicating their key LAB Profile Patterns as well.

I requested that her canvassers write out the answers to my question word-for-word, with no editing. This was important because we wanted to

avoid making any inadvertent changes in the language structure of the respondents' answers.

Here's what we found repeatedly in the responses. Voters stated that at
the moment of decision, what was important to them was that the candidate they would vote for had to have a *deep familiarity* with the community
and its issues. They demanded a *long history of involvement* in community
matters, and made several similar kinds of statements that indicated to me
that the **Sameness** Pattern was the principal LAB Profile Pattern at play.

It was also clear from the language structure that these electors were
not looking for a municipal councilor who would dictate to them or provide instructions to the population at large. In fact, they preferred someone who would *listen to them*. This indicated that the voters at that time
had a fairly **Internal** Pattern. **Now we knew the two Criteria that were
important to them (deep familiarity and involvement in the community)
and the two LAB Profile Patterns that needed to be used in the language
of the campaign.**

I assisted in the design of my friend's campaign marketing materials to
reflect the above Patterns. Having identified the Sameness Pattern as the
LAB Profile element at play, we did our best to highlight her long experience and involvement in the community. Unfortunately, my friend lost
the election. Not surprisingly, given the Sameness Pattern at play, all the
incumbents were returned to power. Despite our best efforts, the results indicated that my friend was still perceived as the "new gal on the block."

The Role of LAB Profile Customer Research

For mass marketing, election campaigns, and other communication strategies, there is a need for a method that is easily usable, effective, and repro-
ducible throughout the organization in branding, in the sales process, and
in marketing communications as well as in staff behavior with customers.

There can be several LAB Profile Patterns at play in the complex interactions between customers and suppliers.

**For some customers, however, there is one driving LAB Profile
Pattern that either makes people purchase services or prevents them
from buying.** For example, the Canadian Automobile Association
(CAA) had a clear example of this. They discovered that people become
members in order to *avoid having problems* when they are traveling by car.
This Away From Pattern was really the only Pattern that mattered for
the customers. For other products and services, you may need a deeper
understanding of how the LAB Profile Patterns affect customers at different points in the buying cycle to determine how best to increase your im-

pact and response rates. While in-depth expertise in LAB Profile and marketing may be needed for a complete Profile of all the buying steps, **you can improve your results in a noticeable way even if you only get one major LAB Profile Pattern right**.

For a mutual fund company client of mine, I interviewed a sample of their high-value customers using an adapted LAB Profile Questionnaire[1] to determine the triggers that drove them to become customers of this particular mutual fund company. Here again, the Context was very important, as was the combination of Patterns. The majority of the customers were highly Internal in the Context of making investment choices; they judged for themselves what was working and wasn't and didn't want to be told what to do, even when they recognized the superior investing expertise in this mutual fund company and in particular its principal.

The clients split into two groups with Options and Procedures. The Options group of investors wanted to have much more choice than the Procedures group. The latter wanted to know there was a method to having their investments taken care of. One element both groups shared was a high Person Pattern. Even though they were highly Internal, they had huge respect for the director of the mutual fund company. He appeared regularly on an investment television show where viewers could call in with their questions about when to buy or sell individual stocks. During my interviews with them, I discovered that they typically watched him on television for a certain period of time (LAB Profile Period of Time) until they were ready to stop making all their individual investment decisions themselves and pass on their portfolios to his company.

It turned out that even though the majority had an Internal preference for deciding where to invest their retirement savings, the **main motivator for starting to think about switching to this mutual fund company was Away From**. It was the fear of not having enough money for their retirement. Many of them followed their own investments daily, and this was in 2007, prior to the market meltdown in 2008. But fear and stress eventually got to them, so they began to follow the results available from my client company to determine whether or not to turn the decision-making over to someone else. **There were several sub-contexts in the decision-making process, and different Patterns became important at different times in the customer's process.**

As a result of this research, I created the sales process to reflect the customers' decision-making processes and the LAB Profile Patterns at play and helped the company use the correct language and visuals for their

---

[1] See Appendix C for a sample questionnaire.

website to support their messages. They were very happy with the resulting increase in customers.

This is the advantage of decoding the customer buying process into LAB Profile Patterns: you can tailor both the marketing and the sales processes to fit the process customers are naturally going through. **This way, you can increase the number of positive responses and decrease the number of potential customers who walk away because of an inadvertent use of the wrong language.**

Attack Campaigns

It has been said that the reason attack advertising continues is because it works. Clearly, attack ads use the Away From Pattern, in an attempt to get voters to move away from a specific candidate. While they may be successful in getting voters to move away, it can be very difficult to control what it is that people move away from. When I was interviewed on television during a particularly negative federal election campaign in Canada, I predicted that the attack approach would so offend many people that they would move away from voting. This was even more salient in the 2008 Canadian federal election, which had the lowest turnout ever at just 59.1%.

In the Canadian cultural context, where the highest held value is to "be nice," attack ads are likely to be a complete turnoff from the whole election process. While I can't be certain that the increase in negative campaigning was the only factor, the number of people participating in that election declined significantly over the last few federal elections.[2] The obvious exception to this trend of using attack advertising was the 2008 American presidential campaign, where the level of debate was raised by Barack Obama and attack advertising was disgraced. That was, until the spring of 2009 when the Canadian Conservative Party, in power with a minority government, once again used attack commercials against the leader of the opposition, Michal Ignatieff, in anticipation of an upcoming federal election.

Direct Marketing

If you want a measurable way to determine what works and what doesn't work in direct marketing, the **LAB Profile Methodology gives you a shortcut for finding and testing your customers' key motivators.** You can

---

[2] Only 60.9% of voters turned out for the 2004 election, down from 64.1% (adjusted) in 2000. Source: http://www.nodice.ca/elections/canada/voterturnout.php. In 2008 the turnout according to Elections Canada was 59.1%.

design direct marketing pieces based on the combination of LAB Profile Patterns your customers have. Customers who are seeking new and different solutions (Difference) and want alternatives (Options) that they themselves can decide about (Internal) can receive a different letter from those customers who are seeking something better (Sameness with Exception) and want to get advice from their supplier (External) as to *how* to go about (Procedures) improving their processes.

Once LAB Profile research has been conducted, you will be able to determine the language needed to reach groups via each channel through which you communicate: telephone, in person, website, e-mail, chat, etc. Measurement and testing will immediately enable you to tweak your use of language for maximum effect.

As all marketers know, the first challenge is to get the customers' attention. In direct marketing, this means getting them to read what you sent them. For this to work, you need to use Difference language and visuals: that is, it needs to be sufficiently different from everything else simply to get their attention.

The second step is to create rapport with the customer and establish your credibility in their eyes. You can reflect their view of an issue, discuss a problem to be solved (Away From), or offer something to be gained (Toward). Here you need to match their Criteria and their likely Toward or Away From Pattern as well as addressing possible objections or reservations about your main message.[3]

Lastly, you need to use the LAB Profile Patterns that you believe are drivers for your clients with regards to their decisions about purchasing your products. **It is vital to clearly and correctly identify the Context and Sub-Contexts of the decision-making process.**

Sometimes there are surprises when you conduct LAB Profile research. David Klaasen, a graduate of the LAB Profile Consultant/Trainer Program, and Dr. Pamela Campanelli, a survey expert, were part of a team running a large LAB Profile research project for a government agency with a very large group of respondents. The original hypothesis was that those who might refuse to reply to the survey would likely have Internal and Away From Patterns in this Context. (The respondents would decide for themselves whether they would avoid participating.) Yet when a large sample of respondents received a letter with the appropriate Internal and Away From language embedded in the text, their response rate was the same as for the control group, which received letters with none of this language. The re-

---

[3] If you do not state your customers' objections upfront, they may not let go of them. For more information on how to overcome your customers' objections, please see my CD or MP3 *Presenting Ideas to Skeptical People*, available from www.WordsThatChangeMinds.com.

sponse was actually lower when the participants' names were used in combination with the Internal and Away From language.

How could this be? **I discussed with them that there are three ways that people can be in Away From mode.** For example, they can be motivated to *avoid a problem* that has yet to occur or to *fix an existing problem*. The third case is where the real question is not "Away From," but "Away From what or whom?" To determine this, it is important to know the respondents' Criteria: that is, what is important to them—their hot buttons, both negative and positive.

As a result of our conversation about this, the team then hypothesized that:[4]

> *Being able to define what sort of Away From the respondents are motivated by can lead us to use subtly different approaches. For example, if they find surveys boring or "not interesting" they may be motivated to avoid getting involved.*
>
> *More significantly if privacy is important, the respondent may be motivated to move away from (prevent) what they believe is an "infringement of privacy" and want to avoid participating, especially if their name is used. Therefore, the more we touched on their below conscious patterns with the LAB Profile the more sensitive they would be to having their name in the letter. It's like they are thinking, "You know too much about me!" This would not be as much about confidentiality as not wanting someone from the government in their home and prying into their personal affairs.*
>
> *The name issue may also have to do with the Person or Thing LAB Profile Patterns. In LAB Profile terms, if someone has a high Person preference in a given Context, then relationships, people, and feelings are important to them. If they have a Thing preference, they concentrate on ideas, tools, tasks, systems, and objects. In the cases where we saw a lower response rate when the individual was named, this could be due to them not wanting a relationship with "the government," and feeling a bit paranoid when the government seemed to know who they were and addressed them by name.*
>
> *So this experiment really illustrates how many complex factors are at play: the various Contexts, Criteria, and the Patterns themselves.*

When you can closely track response rates and identify the Contexts, the respondents' Criteria, and the LAB Profile Influencing Language you

---

[4] Campanelli, P. and Klaasen, D. (2008), "The Language and Behavior Profile as a Nonresponse Tool," paper presented at the 19th International Workshop on Household Survey Nonresponse.

are using, you can create and test direct marketing initiatives and more quickly improve your response rates.[5]

Evaluating Marketing and Advertising Campaigns

The LAB Profile is also a useful tool to evaluate your existing marketing campaigns. You can decode the Patterns inherent in the language used and the visuals. For example, MasterCard used this slogan for many years:

> *"This costs [that much]. That costs [this much]. This costs [that much]. This [thing or event]: priceless.*
>
> *Some things money can't buy; for everything else, there's MasterCard."*

This slogan was extremely successful for MasterCard. Here's how to decode the slogan into LAB Profile terms: the ritualistic or Procedures approach in the repetition of "this costs this much," etc., is followed by the Options twist at the end. "For everything else" is Options language. This slogan thus appealed to both Options and Procedures credit card users. The fact that they used stories in their advertising is a Procedures strategy (all stories are a Procedure in that they have a beginning, a middle, then an end), and they concluded with that little Options flavor at the end of the slogan.

Visa's campaign at the same time differed. For example, one television ad showed a man leaving an expensive camera on a table outside an Italian café and returning to find it the next day, with the tag line:

> *"If life were like that, you wouldn't need a Visa card."*

They had many television ads with the same kind of impossible story and same tag line. In my opinion, this was a very Options-oriented slogan. It was essentially saying that life does not follow a normal standard operating Procedure, and there are nasty surprises that could happen to you. The television commercials did manage to cover some Procedures aspects because there were also storylines in the ads, but even the stories were weird enough to indicate that life does not follow standard Procedure.

I have not conducted any research into the various target markets for Visa or MasterCard, but one thing is clear. The Visa slogan clearly targeted mainly Options preferences, while the MasterCard slogan targeted people with both Procedures and Options preferences.

---

[5] For more information on how language can create behavior change, see Joe Yeager and Linda Sommer's article "Linguistic Mechanisms Cause Rapid Behavior Change, Part Two: How Linguistic Frames Affect Motivation," *The Qualitative Report*, Vol. 12, No. 3, September 2007, pp. 467–82, http://www.nova.edu/ssss/QR/QR12-3/yeager2.pdf.

Customer Relationship Management

The LAB Profile enables you to determine the specific Patterns and sequences of Patterns that your customers have. This can be very useful once integrated into your Customer Relationship Management (CRM) systems.

Imagine asking a telephone customer this Options-Procedures question:

Why did you choose this product today?

You will probably hear either a story (Procedures) or a list of reasons why (Options). You could even gather this information during online sales: record the Pattern in your CRM system, and then call up the specific language that should be used to keep your customer motivated. For your Procedures customers, you can suggest *how to purchase* or *how to use* the item they wish to buy. In the case of an Options-type answer, you can tell them about some of the *other things* this product would do.

The critical Patterns to look for and incorporate into your CRM system as outlined in the Introduction are:

Proactive and Reactive
Toward and Away From
Internal and External
Options and Procedures
Sameness, Sameness with Exception, and Difference
Person and Thing
Convincer Channel (See, Hear, Read, Do) and Convincer Mode
   (Number of Examples, Automatic, Consistent, Period of Time)

Another of my clients is the owner of a Hollywood talent management agency; he works with creative people, mainly television and film script writers. His major LAB Profile Patterns are very Proactive, Toward, Internal, very high Options, and some Procedures. When I communicate with him, I use very short, active sentences (Proactive) and present a couple of alternatives (Options) with a short statement of what each would accomplish (Toward), and then ask him what his opinion is (Internal). This might sound like:

Hey, do you want to decide [Internal] on what else [Options] we can do right now [Proactive] to make this work [Toward]?"

I would not say to him:

Let's think through thoroughly [Reactive] how we have to proceed [Procedures] before doing anything [more Reactive] in case we make a mistake [Away From].

The Methodology Exists: Why Miss the Opportunity?

The methodology for understanding customers and managing customer relationships has now existed for some time. Why wouldn't everyone take the time and effort to truly understand their customers? **It is a wasted opportunity to continue to develop products and services without incorporating what motivates your customers for each channel through which they contact you or through which you contact them.**

As described in earlier sections, you can manage your client's experience every time they are in contact with your organization by creating the right customer philosophy, having the appropriate normal transaction process, and using the Words That Change Minds Upset Customer Process, all based on a firm grasp of the customer's main LAB Profile Patterns. You can make sure that this experience is complete by using this knowledge to create marketing that fits your customer's precise motivations. Plus you can hire and train your staff to match . . . but that is in the next chapter.

CHAPTER 13

Recruiting for Positive Relationships

It is critically important to choose the right people to serve and sell to your customers. When you choose the right people to begin with, then training them, getting them up to speed, and ensuring they treat customers the way you want are practically assured. It is essential to avoid hiring the wrong people; ultimately, they will cost you money and create frustration, as you try to create the kind of experience you want your customers to have. When you have recruited the right people for your organization, getting them up to speed is easier, they won't behave as if the customer is bothering them, and they are unlikely to pass the buck or blame others at those critical moments when meeting the customer's needs has the biggest impact on their willingness to continue to be a customer. **When your sales and service staff have the appropriate LAB Profile, your customer philosophy will be delivered by people who not only believe it, they live it.**

The LAB Profile is a tool that will help you hire for fit, not knowledge or skill. You can attract and select only the people who fit the environment and the tasks you need them to accomplish, including the kind of relationships you wish them to be able to establish.

Because the LAB Profile enables you to understand people based on their below-conscious Motivation Triggers, you can first analyze a position and decode it into the critical Triggers. Then, using the appropriate Influencing Language, you can describe the job in a way that only attracts the people who fit. When this is done well, your advertisement will usually also turn off the people who will not fit. This is an excellent way of reducing your recruitment costs by reducing the number of candidates who apply, while increasing the number of candidates who fit.[1]

You can also use the LAB Profile to select members of project teams and other groups where performance is critical and fit is the deciding fac-

---

[1] There are LAB Profile-based online tools that can assist companies with hiring for fit. Check out www.jobEQ.com, www.IWAMinstitute.com and www.Identity-Compass.com.

tor. Of course, when hiring and selecting, you need to make sure that your short-listed candidates have the appropriate knowledge and skill base. What the LAB Profile can do is help you pick the best candidate according to what motivates them, how they think, and how well suited they are for the tasks and relationships at hand.

Preparing a Job Profile

In order to profile a position, you will need information about the job itself, the environment (current situation and history), and the culture (nature of the team or organization) in which the successful candidate will be working. For the position itself, you will need to understand the purpose of the position and the specific tasks and responsibilities that the person will hold. For any potential position, take the time to fill out Forms 13-1 and 13-2 on Motivation and Working Traits as a start to help you determine the profile of a job. As you can see, each Pattern is a on a continuum. You can rate a job description as one Pattern or the other . . . or somewhere in between.

Creating Customer Service and Sales Profiles for Recruiting[2]

Use Forms 13-1 and 13-2 to help you clarify where on each continuum the ideal candidate for a specific job should fall. We can make some general statements about certain positions. Where the job consists mainly of order taking, problem solving, and directing phone traffic to the correct person, the typical LAB Profile of these kinds of customer service positions necessitates that the people be a little Reactive, very Person, and mainly Procedures. This will ensure that your staff do not descend on the customers like vultures looking for fresh meat, but will be attentive to the people and able to follow the correct process.

If you hire overly Proactive people for many service positions, they are unlikely to stay in the job very long or be willing to sit at their desks receiving phone calls. If they have a very Thing orientation and not enough of a Person preference, they are unlikely to establish the kind of relationship with the customer that you need.

There are many exceptions to these general ideas, so it is important to analyze the work that needs to be done. In a crisis center or emergency

---

[2] It takes some analysis to create the ideal Profile for a position. There are more instructions on how to do this in my first book, *Words That Change Minds*, on pp. 163–7. Alternatively, you could work with a Certified LAB Profile Consultant/Trainer. On www.WordsThatChangeMinds.com, you can find someone in your area.

Form 13-1 — Motivation Traits Position Analysis

Does the job demand that the person:

LEVEL:

Proactive		Reactive
Just go and do it	Think and do it	Think about it

DIRECTION:

Toward		Away From
Manage priorities Focus on goals	Focus on priorities and prevent problems	Identify, prevent, and solve problems

SOURCE:

Internal		External
Decide by oneself Hold standards	Decide and adapt	Adapt to feedback

REASON:

Procedures		Options
Follow procedures	Follow and adapt procedures	Create procedures, find alternatives

DECISION FACTORS:

Difference	Sameness with Exception	Sameness
Revolution, frequent change	Evolution	Maintain status quo

Form 13-2 provides the same type of working form for those Working Traits you are looking for in a potential job candidate.

Form 13-2—Working Traits

Which of the following are important in this position?

SCOPE:

General		Specific
Big picture	Overview and detail	Detail

ATTENTION DIRECTION:

Other	Self
Rapport with others	Exclusive focus on content

STRESS RESPONSE:

Feelings	Choice	Thinking
Low stress	Medium stress	High stress

STYLE:

Independent	Proximity	Cooperative
Work alone	In charge of own territory with others around	Work together as a group

ORGANIZATION:

Person		Thing
Focus on people and relationships	People and tasks	Tasks to be accomplished

RULE STRUCTURE:

My-My	No-My	My/.	My-Your
Communicate rules and expectations	Transmit received rules	Just get it done	Understand both sides

CONVINCER CHANNEL:

See	Hear	Read	Do
See evidence	Listen	Read	Work with

CONVINCER MODE:

Number of Examples	Automatic	Consistent	Period of Time
Separate examples	Know right away	Hard to convince	Convinced over time

department in a hospital, for example, where people are speaking with and handling calls for people who are experiencing an emergency, it is useful to hire people who have a combination of mainly Thing with some Person. This combination will help them have empathy with the client or patient while at the same time keeping their focus on solving the crisis rather than getting caught up in it.

For front-line reception and order-taking positions, I recommend hiring people with a Person Pattern, combined with a mainly Procedures Pattern. The reason I suggest a mainly Procedures Pattern rather than a totally Procedures one is that you want the person to follow a process without rigidly sticking to it. Should the customer need something else to occur, this Profile allows enough flexibility to switch into the Words That Change Minds Upset Customer Process. Ideally, for these front-line positions the Stress Response Pattern needs to be Choice. This means that a person is likely to feel empathy, but is still able to choose what to do next as appropriate.

The Choice Pattern will enable your front-line people to have empathy for the people who contact them and still be able to step out of the emotional realm easily in order to meet their needs. For both front-line contact center and in-person positions, it is important to avoid hiring someone with the Stress Response Pattern of Feelings, because when something goes wrong, they will have an enormous emotional reaction and may stay stuck in that negative emotional state and have difficulty regaining their equilibrium.

For retail sales positions, some of the above Patterns will also be important. Everyone has had the experience of being pounced upon by Proactive retail salespeople. However, if the retail salespeople are too Reactive, they tend not to be around at the time when the customer needs them, because they don't notice when they need to take the initiative.

Great Universal Shopping
HIRING SUCCESS STORY

Great Universal Shopping (GUS) in the United Kingdom has the largest call center in the UK and the third largest in Europe. Most of their contact center employees are women who work part-time. A graduate from the LAB Profile Consultant/Trainer Certification Program, who was the HR manager, used the LAB Profile to model their top performers. When I visited one contact center, I noticed that the cubicles were all shoulder height, so that each employee could see above and around to the other people—an uncommon practice, in my experience.

As I entered the room, I noticed that most of the employees lifted their eyes to watch me come in while they maintained their phone conversations with their customers. Almost everybody greeted me with a smile, a nod, and a twinkling of their eyes. I was overwhelmed by how welcoming, friendly, and curious these women were. Can you guess their driving LAB Profile Pattern? It was Person. Plus, they had the ability to split their attention and multi-task, since they had to follow a complicated screen during their work as well as maintain rapport with their customers.

As part of the consulting I did for them, I sat in to listen to their top performer. Her job was to confirm the orders that people had placed, let them know which products were in stock, and, if the products they wanted were not currently in stock, offer other products of a similar nature and upsell if the opportunity arose. What was amazing about this staff member was her ability to instantly create rapport with the customer.

I remember one call in particular. The automatic dialer called the number and the screen showed the order that had been placed. When the customer picked up the phone, the employee identified herself as a GUS employee and said the purpose of her call was to confirm the customer's order. **The female customer had an irritated tone of voice and replied that she didn't have a lot of time, as she was packing to go away on a vacation.** This is what followed:

> **GUS employee:** Oh! Where are you going?
>
> **Customer:** We're leaving tomorrow in our caravan [camper] with friends and I have a lot to do.
>
> **GUS employee:** Really? That sounds wonderful! Do you have everything you need to go away tomorrow?
>
> **Customer:** Well now, I don't actually.

The customer then proceeded to reel off a list of items that she needed right away. The GUS employee had most of those items couriered to the customer, for arrival early the next morning before the woman left on vacation. The staff member's interest in people enabled her to have a real conversation with her customer, the benefit of which was that she was able to uncover other needs that weren't part of the original purpose for the call.

I asked this employee how she used the computer script that was supposed to guide her from screen to screen. **She told me that the script was really only for when she was having a bad day, and the most important thing was to be of help to the customer**. Don't you wish that every service person you spoke to had the same attitude?

Writing Ads to Attract the Right People

GUS had a great employment ad. They advertised in the local papers closest to their contact centers. They had a picture of a woman on the phone looking professional with the tag line:

Do you like talking to your friends on the phone?
Have we got the job for you!

Because the Person Pattern was so fundamental to the success of this job, they designed their recruitment ads specifically to attract people with this Pattern. The picture of the woman was a visual example of a Person Pattern, while the words attracted people who were already comfortable establishing rapport with people on the phone.

Irish Continental Group

CASE STUDY[3]

In 1999, Irish Ferries, the car ferry operation of Irish Continental Group Ltd., was in a difficult competitive situation with Stena Lines, a Swedish company. In the key Dublin to Hollyhead, UK route, Stena had a competitive advantage with a faster, more comfortable ferry. Irish Ferries took the risk of competing against Stena with a less comfortable boat. They decided to focus on creating a particular customer experience, instead of competing on traditional grounds of fare or better amenities.

Human Resources Director Brendan McCarthy (a graduate of the LAB Profile Consultant/Trainer Certification Program) was the business leader for this campaign. In his opinion:

Repeat business is absolutely critical in the car passenger business (most important in terms of volumes and margins). In general terms, nearly 75% (350,000 cars in total) of business came from [less than 9%] 40,000 cars. On-board sales operate from very high margins. Therefore, if you could get new customers on board and transfer them into repeat customers, it would have a disproportionately positive effect on the bottom line, given that fixed costs were high and the marginal cost of adding additional cars is very low.

Most of Irish Ferries' research had suggested that the biggest influence was "word-of-mouth." The objective, therefore, was to create an experience for the customer that increased the likelihood of repeat business, positive word-of-mouth, and a role model for the rest of the company. A great opportunity existed. So, in 2000, they invested in a new ferry and named it the *Jonathan Swift,*[4] and here is what they did next.

---

[3] This case study was generously contributed by Certified LAB Profile Consultant/Trainer Brendan McCarthy based on his experience as human resources director for Irish Continental Group.
[4] The name of the vessel has a lovely double meaning: both the world-renowned author of *Gulliver's Travels* and the word "Swift" to give speed to its name.

The Jonathan Swift Process

Irish Ferries' first step was to research what their customers wanted and then set up all the pieces to create that particular experience.

1.   Identify what really satisfied customers would be saying about their experience.
     (a)   What type of service and services would contribute to these customer perceptions?
     (b)   What behaviors on the part of the staff would make the customer feel this way?
2.   Identify what types of people in LAB Profile terms are most likely to display the behaviors listed in (a) and (b) and find ways of attracting people with the right LAB Profile Language.
3.   Set up a staff selection procedure that not only identified the "right type," but also gave a first impression of the company that was consistent with the sought-after mood and behavior.
4.   Create an environment that was conducive to the "right Profile" and satisfied staff's needs in order to ensure that the right staff members would stay.
5.   Develop leadership competencies and values consistent with this approach.
6.   Be passionate about the company's beliefs and demonstrate it in their behavior.

Based on their research, they decided that the customer experience would be designed around customer enjoyment. This included entertainment activities for children and a jazz band, as well as an interior design with flexible tables and seating arrangements that could be adapted for various activities.

People were the focus of Human Resources Director Brendan McCarthy's strategy. He knew that it would be essential to have passengers have such a good time that they would be happy to forgo the benefits of the quicker, more comfortable ride that the competition delivered. The layout, food, and environment would all be important in this, but the most important difference would be the people working both aboard the ship and on the ground.

People Strategy

As I explained in Chapter 5, it is important to identify your organization's philosophy so you can create a plan of action to implement it on every level. Irish Ferries started with just that: they identified the philosophy by which they would hire and manage the staff to create the desired result of customer enjoyment. As illustrated in this example, making the effort to create their philosophy enabled them to focus all their activities to achieve the one important aim: customer enjoyment.

The People Philosophy

1. Create a story representing what you are trying to achieve.
2. Identify what must be done to obtain this result.
3. Be specific as to the LAB Profile Patterns most likely to create the desired behaviors.
4. Let this be the critical issue in selecting staff.
5. Engage in ongoing ceremonies and celebrations to reinforce desired behaviors.
6. Create an environment that delivers on staff personal and professional fulfillment needs (based on desired LAB Profile).
7. Give staff constant feedback on how they're doing.
8. "Workouts," free open discussion on staff's agenda (these were regular meetings with the business manager solely on the staff's agenda).
9. Encourage staff to color outside the lines in their own behavior.
10. One-on-one meetings with all staff monthly.

Here is Brendan's description[5] for the people they wanted to hire:

- The emphasis will be on "customer enjoyment" rather than simple customer satisfaction. Staff should set out to ensure that passengers have a "good time" on board the vessel, creating an environment where customers have a "fun" experience in keeping with the start of an "Irish Holiday" (or other holiday for Irish passengers).
- There should be a strong emphasis on proactive customer interactions, with staff taking the initiative in helping passengers get the most enjoyment from their journey.
- Staff should be "personalities"—friendly, natural, outgoing, and gregarious. They should enjoy mixing with people and perform more as "party hosts" rather than as passenger servants. They should be willing and skilled at putting passengers at ease, engaging them in conversation, telling jokes, intuiting passenger interests, and encouraging something of a party atmosphere.
- Staff should have a natural liking for children as well as an affinity for elderly people.
- They should have a good knowledge of transport and facilities at both ports, and be ready and able to offer suggestions to passengers, which will help passengers further enjoy their holidays.
- Staff should be proactive in thinking up ways of improving the service, both individually and collectively. They will regularly get together to review their performance and swap ideas for improvement. Their ideas will range from how to make their day-to-day duties and customer contacts more effective, how to defuse disgruntled passengers, and how to keep kids occupied, right through to generating ideas for making the "party" more successful and enjoyable.

---

[5] All information is presented here with permission.

- Staff are expected to be knowledgeable about the vessel and proud to explain its many features.
- They will also be a highly professional sales force, encouraging passengers to spend money, staying alert to selling opportunities, up-selling and cross-selling, and, in fact, being quite entrepreneurial in their approach.
- Staff will be motivated by their own and each other's enthusiasm for the job. More importantly, they will be motivated by the gratitude and enjoyment of the passengers. They will be sympathetic to disgruntled passengers and will have the behavioral and verbal skills to correct difficult situations.
- They will take their jobs to heart, and most likely will spend off-duty hours thinking about how they can make things more enjoyable for their passengers.

The LAB Profile for Customer Enjoyment Staff

Having identified the attitudes and behaviors they wanted their staff to have, the next step for Irish Ferries was to identify the key LAB Profile Patterns they wanted to find in their staff. There were about 150 people hired through this process. The following lists the criteria Human Resources staff identified as ideal before they began the interview process.

Criteria

Candidates will generally be outgoing and at ease with people. They will have a good sense of humor, and will find it easy to converse with other people at all levels. Their attention will be focused on other people, which will allow them to respond quickly and naturally and to follow or lead conversations. In interpersonal dealings they will tend to be proactive, usually initiating conversations rather than waiting to respond to someone else. Through their attention to other people and their (usually) unconscious observance of body language and behavioral detail, they will have developed an almost instinctive understanding of what other people are likely to need or want to do.

Direction (Toward/Away From)—Mainly Away From

Candidates will be good at anticipating difficulties and finding solutions, paying attention to what might go wrong or what might need fixing, especially with regard to other people. Their ears will prick up when someone tells them they have a problem, and they will feel almost compelled to respond. They will be motivated by deadlines because they have a need to avoid the difficulties that could occur when they're not met. This will equip them to deal with fast turnarounds. They may have some aspirations toward achievement, but will usually put these aside if there's something that has to be solved.

Source (Internal/External)—Mainly External

Candidates will tend to rely on the opinions of others in order to make decisions, and will often ask for suggestions about what they should do or how they should respond. They will enjoy getting positive feedback from passengers and their superiors, and will usually be motivated by this. They will also tend to be quite ready to give positive feedback to others. However, they will be able to evaluate negative feedback and decide for themselves whether or not it's justified. They will be sympathetic to passenger complaints, but where these are out of their control, they won't let themselves become personally affected.

Reason (Options/Procedures)—Mainly Procedures

Candidates will be careful to observe established procedures and will tend to look for the "right" way of doing things. Once started on a procedure, they will usually feel compelled to finish it. However, their need to help people will occasionally lead them to look for ways to bend the rules, especially if they know they will get positive feedback and appreciation.

Decision Factors (Sameness/Sameness with Exception/Difference)—Sameness with Exception

Candidates will work best in an environment where there is steady and sustained improvement. They will look for better ways of doing things and will respond to changes that are progressively implemented. They will prefer things that are better or improved rather than new or different. They will be uncomfortable with change, which is perceived as being revolutionary. Equally, they will quickly become unhappy if they think things are staying the same.

Scope (General/Specific)—Mainly General

Candidates will have a good general sense of their jobs and how their individual roles fit into the overall picture. This general overview will also help them adapt to a wide variety of tasks and allow them to understand their importance. They will also have a good sense of detail for their own work areas and will be aware if little things are not right. However, they will need to be reminded of the big picture to maintain their focus.

Attention Direction (Self/Other)—Other

Candidates will tend to pay attention to the comfort and well-being of others before they attend to their own. In conversations and in group situations, they will be adept at reading people's emotions and body language, and will usually make most sense of people's communications through nonverbal messages. They will understand the content of people's messages, but will weigh this against what they consider to be the feelings of the people they are dealing with. They will tend to respond automatically to other people's needs rather than wait to be asked to do things.

Style (Independent/Proximity/Cooperative)—Mainly Cooperative

Candidates will enjoy working with other people and being part of a team. They will understand that there is a need for people to have defined areas of responsibility, but they will often overlook this in order to help others get things done. They will become uncomfortable if they have to work for long periods by themselves.

Rule Structure—My/Your

Candidates will have a good sense of what they need to do, but will usually let circumstances dictate how they should perform their tasks and the priorities they should follow. They will usually accept that others may wish to do things in a different way than them. They will not have any rules or expectations of how customers should behave.

Irish Ferries felt that it was not enough to hire people that were the right fit or had the right inclination to create customer enjoyment. They also knew it was important to support these people by having an environment supporting people with the above-mentioned Patterns. The following are what Brendan McCarthy calls key practices regarding the work environment.

Key Practices

According to Brendan McCarthy, the following are the key practices or issues that made the difference in creating the ideal work environment:

1. The uniform was designed for ease of wear, comfort while working, and general appeal to the staff.
2. Numerous methods of gaining customer feedback were used (letters, surveys, visitors' book, anecdotal comments recorded by staff, etc.) and the night staff were organized into groups to analyze, interpret, brainstorm ideas, and make proposals.
3. The "workout" concept was used whereby staff held regular meetings with the business manager solely on the staff's agenda.
4. The concept of one-on-ones, [where] the manager and the staff member shared their assessments on how they were "showing up for each other." A strong relationship and deep understanding of each other's position resulted. This was conducted against the backdrop of the "story" of who we were and what we were trying to achieve.

Brendan headed up the *Jonathan Swift* program for about a year after it was introduced. During that time, he invested a lot of his time in searching for opportunities to give staff positive feedback on specific observed behaviors consistent with the company's desired goals. He also made coaching the leaders a very high priority. The impact the leaders and managers had in motivating and encouraging staff was key. These activities were seen as critical to the "means of achieving" the goal of profitability. Traditionally, the focus would have been on the end itself.

Irish Ferries was also attentive to their customer philosophy and made a strategic decision to combine three purposes for customer feedback mechanisms. **Their customer feedback processes were designed to help customers:**

- Focus on what they liked about the experience
- State what they would tell others about their experience
- Identify areas for improvement

This was a fully integrated part of their strategy.
Brendan McCarthy comments:

Conventional Customer surveys or Comment Cards may point people in the direction of negative aspects of their experiences. They may even bring to the attention of the individual completing the survey negative aspects of the experience that they may not have been previously aware of until asked. When asked a question such as "how clean was the room, etc." indirectly one is being asked to see if they can now find dirt. As such, an individual may be more aware of faults after completing the questionnaire and it is this view that they are more likely to emphasize when speaking to others about their experience.

Instead of promoting the "negative" aspects, it is possible to elicit valuable information while at the same time leaving the person completing the survey with a more positive attitude and disposition towards the company. The point is to ensure that the customers comment on their experience in such a way that leaves them feeling better and more likely to be positive ambassadors for the company.

Results

The plan was successful. In 2000, in an overall static market, Irish Ferries achieved a 6.7% increase in passenger vehicles carried on the Dublin-Holyhead route in the year to October. From October 2000 onward, the new ferry experienced continuing strong growth—62% over the same period in the previous year. They were even able to get a slight premium on fares: for example, a five-day return fare for a car with two passengers was £169, against the competitive fare on Stena Lines' fast ferry of £159.[6]

In 2001, after the September 11 events, when the total passenger numbers fell by 6% within the company, the numbers traveling on the *Jonathan Swift* actually increased by 11%.

Customer feedback (letters, surveys, logbook entries, and anecdotal feedback) was given to staff to brainstorm on and come up with ideas for improvement. During that year, customer feedback by way of unsolicited letters was very complimentary of the staff, giving specific quotes of how the staff had gone above and beyond the call of duty. **On the conventional ferries, complimentary letters accounted for less than 2% of those received, whereas for the *Jonathan Swift*, 70% of letters received were complimentary.**

For Brendan McCarthy, the icing on the cake was the good humor of the staff and their levels of energy and excitement. He stated:

"The staff were capable, aligned to the customer-first philosophy and how to achieve it and intrinsically motivated to naturally think and behave as required. They wanted to and gave of their best. You could see this in the faces and eyes of the staff and in the numerous examples of what they did in their own time with the customers, such as taking them on tours of Dublin, etc."

Because of Irish Ferries' attention in conducting the whole hiring process, customers could palpably sense the staff's complete commitment to creating an enjoyable experience for them. Irish Continental Group Ltd., through their human resources director and his team, focused on the following:

- Creating their customer philosophy and customer experience goals from the customer's point of view
- Identifying their people philosophy, which focused on the key activities staff needed to do to fulfill the customer philosophy
- Identifying the right LAB Profile Patterns that their staff needed to have to naturally undertake the key activities
- Designing a physical and social environment conducive to both the desired customer experience and supporting staff with the right LAB Profile
- Organizing innovative ongoing feedback from customers and to and from staff to ensure continued alignment and adjustments when needed

---

The *Jonathan Swift* process is an A to Z example of how to design the experience you want your customers to have. It all starts with decid-

---

[6] These results were reported by Ken Irons in a report entitled *How Superservice Brought a Thousand Welcomes to the Irish Sea*, Insead, Fontainebleau, March 2001.

ing what kind of company you want to be and then taking that identity all the way through your organization. That's what we cover next in Chapter 14, "From Branding to Behavior." Chapter 15 contains the next steps: the exercises and resources for team leaders to help their staff develop the kinds of behaviors in the Words That Change Minds Customer Transaction Process and Upset Customer Process.

CHAPTER 14

From Branding to Behavior

When you want to fully incorporate a deep understanding of your clients throughout your entire operation, you can use the LAB Profile, the Words That Change Minds Customer Transaction Process, and the Words That Change Minds Upset Customer Process to:

- Ensure that what you do and say both internally to employees and externally to customers reflects your company identity and Customer Philosophy: in other words, how to take your branding and make sure it shows up in staff behavior
- Enable you to continue to improve your processes by using naturally occurring feedback and improvement mechanisms

The basic technical mechanisms for doing both of these exist. Customer Relationship Management (CRM) software can be adapted to input individual customer LAB Profile Patterns. Unified communication systems linking phone, Internet, intranet, and e-mail enable seamless communication between all parts of the organization and give greater facility to communicate with customers.[1]

The missing piece consists of integrating similarly advanced psychology for understanding and influencing customers. There have been attempts to do this. Demographics are now recognized as insufficient for understanding the deeper needs of customers, and predictive psychological

---

[1] Wikipedia cites the benefits: "Unified communications helps businesses, small and large alike, to streamline information delivery and ensure ease of use. Human delays are also minimized or eliminated, resulting in better, faster interaction and service-delivery for the customer, and cost savings for the business. Unified communications also allows for easier, more direct collaboration between co-workers and with suppliers and clients, even if they are not physically on the same site."

models often produce fairly soft, opinion-laced data and are insufficient in decoding complex motivations.[2]

Instead, the LAB Profile can be integrated into organizational communication systems to facilitate communicating with individual customers from anyone and to anyone. You can then use these systems to track and record customer preferences. For example, for highly Procedural customers, you can give them a clear process to follow, or for Options customers, a note to propose alternatives and to look at "what else" they need. For Away From customers, you can systematically show them how to prevent problems from happening; for Difference customers, you can let them know what is new. When you integrate the gathering of LAB Profile preferences into your sales and service processes, you can give the customer exactly what they want and avoid accidentally turning them off.

Additionally, you can figure out which LAB Profile Patterns underlie your branding and then ensure that these Patterns are an integral part of your customer communication and service.

From Branding to Behavior

The LAB Profile helps ensure the qualities you identified for your branding are carried right through to sales and customer service staff behavior. If your branding is all about possibilities and the sky's the limit with huge potential (Options), you will want to make sure that your staff are living the brand. Training staff to probe deeper in determining *what else* customers want, to talk about *other possibilities*, and to reassure the customer that what she wants is truly *possible* would be strongly indicated in this type of environment.

If your branding is all about being the "Masters of How" (Procedures), your people need to use the word "how" as they talk to customers. They need to let the customer know that staff can show them *how* the products or services will enable them to do something and that the company has a *procedure* for doing just that. Take Home Depot's slogan:

You can do it. We can help.

It is an example of a *masters of how* branding.

---

[2] In two of his insightful papers, "Databases Don't Measure Motivation" and "Innovative Motivational Profiling: Comparing Marketing Projective Techniques Versus Linguistic Forensic Techniques," Joseph Yeager, Ph.D. points out that even sophisticated quantitative databases that describe or follow people's behavior on the Internet provide at best unreliable guesses to future behavior. He argues for the use of experimental *linguistic* motivational profiling tools. He has developed his own methodology, using NLP and the LAB Profile (among others) and a proprietary method for gathering and using motivational profiling. See his articles in *The Qualitative Report*, Vol. 10, No. 1, March 2005, at pp. 163–77 (http://www.nova.edu/ssss/QR/QR10-1/yeager.pdf), and *The Qualitative Report*, Vol. 8, No. 1, June 2003, at pp. 129–50 (http://www.nova.edu/ssss/QR/QR8-1/yeager.pdf).

If your branding is about removing a headache from your customers, you need to use that language. ING Bank advertises the "Unmortgage" and has slogans such as:

Money doesn't grow on fees.
Saving money shouldn't cost you money.

They could follow this up with their website language and customer service call center staff, sprinkling their vocabulary with sentences like "The new tax saving account will allow you to reduce your taxes" or "Here's how to avoid paying service charges."

Lawson Software, which develops, sells, and implements enterprise management systems, uses this slogan:

Simpler is better.

Their slogan, at a below-conscious level, has two Sameness with Exception words: it's all about progressive change—improving, not throwing the baby out with the bathwater and trying to change everything. They have matched this language in their online marketing by using the same kind of vocabulary to show their customers how to *add* value, *grow* business, and be *stronger*.

L'Oréal Paris has had movie stars telling their clients for years:

Because you're worth it.

This is language aimed at people who are External to the movie stars and External about their appearance, so they have the star telling (Command Language) women to value themselves. More recently, L'Oréal has given the slogan a little makeover, but one that makes a big difference. Now the movie star says:

Because I'm worth it.

This is an invitation (Language of Suggestion) to be like the movie star; it appeals more to people who are Internal about their appearance, those who will decide for themselves if they want to follow the example of the movie star. The question is: who really is their audience, women who are in External or Internal mode with regards to purchasing beauty products? Only their hairdresser knows for sure!

Each of these organizations can ensure a certain kind of customer experience by taking the underlying patterns behind their branding and slogans to make sure this experience is reflected all through the organization, every time the customer has contact with them. They also need to have a means to ensure they can easily improve customer experience, as discussed in the next section.

Simpler Continual Improvement Systems

Organizations that are committed to continually improving what they deliver to their customers can empower their front line as primary information getters.[3] A system can be set up to monitor e-mail feedback and complaints, while contact center staff and front-line in-person staff can be given the means to input raw data for analysis.

When a complaint comes over the counter, for example, the front-line staff person could explain to the customer:

We want to make sure that we understand exactly what the issue is because we are collecting information in order to improve our systems.

If a template is available, the staff member can then record the type of complaint and exactly what went wrong and any suggestions available from the customer. These comments, complaints, and suggestions can then be forwarded to a person responsible for collecting the data and analyzing the trends. **This is a fast, low-cost way to create great responsiveness to off-the-cuff input from customers.** It is very important to capture this kind of information directly from customers, because it accurately reflects the customer's experience in real time. Unfortunately, surveys provide less accurate information because they inevitably occur at times when the customer is not having an immediate experience.

Let the customer know that their data are going to be analyzed so that the organization can respond, and that while a specific solution to the overall problem cannot be guaranteed, this is the best way the customer can help the company provide what they really want and avoid having the same kinds of issues come up in the future.

I believe this methodology is much more effective and particularly more cost-effective than conducting customer surveys. **Another problem with surveys is that the organization will only ask the questions the organization wants to know about when it wants to know, whereas when you encourage spontaneous customer input, you find out what is important to customers from their point of view at that specific time.** You may find out things you don't want to hear this way, but these things may be beneficial to overall continual improvement.

---

[3] See also Chapter 5, "Create Your Customer Philosophy to Sell More"—Automatic Feedback Mechanisms and Triggers of Change Mechanisms as part of your organization's Customer Philosophy.

Building Feedback into Your Improvement System: Triggers of Change Mechanisms

If you have in place the technological and communication systems you want to establish with your customers and your sales and customer service staff, it is critically important to ensure that these systems enable you to implement your unique Triggers of Change Mechanisms. As discussed in Chapter 5, in developing your Customer Philosophy, **Triggers of Change Mechanisms are the processes organizations use to decide *at what point* they will review and/or correct a process.** How many times does a problem for a customer have to occur before you fix it? If you are going to create a wonderful customer experience matched to your brand and your Customer Philosophy and roll it out throughout the organization, then you will probably want to have a system to pick up and analyze feedback and subsequently make decisions about what to do to improve products, services, and the customer experience.

It works easiest when you receive feedback from customers automatically as they do business with you, without having to conduct formal surveys or use feedback cards.[4] Receiving automatic feedback is a critical part of continually improving the system, but unless you have a commitment to reviewing or changing any part of your system, this automatic feedback may be worse than a waste of time. It may harm your reputation with your customers, who will expect that when they are asked for their opinions, something will happen as a result.

You can decide on Triggers of Change Mechanisms for your organization as a whole, or each team can do this for themselves in a more decentralized organization. **First, determine how you will gather information from your customers about their experience doing business with you.** How will you know if there are unintended obstacles that make it harder to purchase or get service? On Air Canada's website, there is an option to offset your personal carbon footprint[5] by paying a small fee. Unfortunately, when you click on this option, you have to leave their website and re-input all your personal and payment data. But there is no comment page to tell Air Canada about how inconvenient this is, so they are unlikely to find out about this nuisance factor, which is a deterrent to purchasing.

Secondly, someone will need to analyze the information coming in from your Automatic Feedback Mechanisms and make a recommendation as to when and if you need to make an improvement or change an element

---

[4] See also Chapter 5, "Create Your Customer Philosophy to Sell More"—Automatic Feedback Mechanisms.

[5] The carbon emissions you are responsible for creating by taking a flight.

of your sales and service systems. Typically this will involve some trial and error and a rigorous evaluation of costs and benefits to customers. **Remember to check each point of view—your own, your customer's, and the fly-on-the-wall—to get every perspective before making a decision.** The fly-on-the-wall perspective enables you to also take into account the future consequences of your decisions. For example, if you decide that maintaining a help line is not worth the cost because few customers have been using it, think about the products and services that may be introduced in the future. Are your customers likely to need help with those new products and services? From the customer's point of view, are you likely to be viewed as cheap because the help line no longer exists?

The airline Easyjet at one point "improved" their website, but clearly not from their customers' point of view. They have added several other options to booking your flight. Now they assume you want to buy travel insurance, and unless you look very carefully and check three separate screens, whether you want it or not, you will be charged for insurance. Getting rid of the insurance consists of first clicking a small button to say you don't want it. This brings you to a new page where they leave the option on, but ask whether you are sure and list several reasons why you really should take insurance. After you click on the "no" button on this page and then click "continue," you will find the insurance is still on your bill! To remove it, you need to *return* to the second page, ensure the "no" button is still clicked, and then click on the "update" button.

Very tricky! It leaves a bad taste in the customer's mouth. The organization failed to consider the impact of these changes on customer perceptions. What with the insurance glitch and the sudden addition of a significant fee for checking luggage, the customers may begin to question whether the company can be trusted.

When you have Automatic Feedback and a Trigger of Change Mechanism that evaluates possible decisions from all three points of view, you avoid the typical problem of large organizations that have become too Internal. When faced with changing outside demands, their tendency is to dismiss any feedback that does not match what they already think: inflexibility in action. When staff spend more time meeting bureaucratic demands than they do meeting customer expectations, the organization has become too Internal and Procedural and not responsive enough (External) to actual and potential customers.

I was recently traveling in the Paris Metro when the train came to a halt at a station. We waited for a couple of minutes, and then the driver announced that there was a problem many stations down the line and he would inform us as soon as he knew anything. What a pleasant surprise. He kept us updated every five minutes by telling us what was going on. Apparently a passenger was unwell and medical services had to be called. Many of the passengers in my car were riveted to the story and stayed to hear the ending rather than leaving to find another way to get where they were going. In total, the story and the wait took 20 minutes. The driver ended the story by telling us that the passenger was conscious and being taken away by a team of medics to a hospital for further tests. He thanked us for our patience, and we were on our way. I recounted this event to several of my Parisian friends and they said this behavior was unusual, but we all agreed on how desirable it is.

The necessary technology and methodologies exist to integrate feedback from customers and to track information about their different motivations (using the LAB Profile or other profiling techniques) and the responses they need from you. The challenge is the same one that IT departments still face: integrating legacy systems and procedures into a congruent, flowing system that is ready for future developments because it continually solicits and adapts to feedback. The most important element in creating a brand with aligned customer messages and slogans, ensuring the right behaviors throughout the organization, is having the will to do it from the very top. Once the will is there, anything is possible, even surviving and thriving through the worst disasters.

Maple Leaf Foods and the Listeria Outbreak of 2008

CASE STUDY

The president and CEO of Maple Leaf Foods, Michael McCain, definitely had a customer focus when a listeriosis outbreak was traced to Maple Leaf meat packing facilities in the summer of 2008. "We had to take the most conservative approach possible . . . and recalled 100% of the production from the entire facility," said McCain at that time. The company also paid to air public service announcements on television to warn Canadians. McCain calculated that the recall would cost the company about $20 million, about 10 times more than originally estimated.[6] Tragically twenty-one people lost their lives from listeriosis poisoning. The company worked closely with federal investigators to determine the cause and correct the issues. As of March 2009, a class-action settlement had been approved by the courts. "It's blindingly clear that Maple Leaf was responsible for the loss of 21 lives," McCain told a meeting of the *Toronto Star* editorial board. "I felt that personally." While Maple Leaf conducted its own internal listeria tests prior to the outbreak, McCain said the company had not been rigorous enough

---

[6] As reported by CBC News, August 25, 2008.

about analyzing the results. "We didn't have a sense of what was high," he said. "We weren't asking the government for more rigorous standards. We should have been."[7]

In spite of the fact that 21 people had lost their lives to listeriosis and many others had became ill, the reputation of Maple Leaf Foods did not suffer much afterwards, because Michael McCain did the right things. He acknowledged the issue immediately upon discovery, took precautions to destroy inventory that might have been harmful, helped with the investigation, and at all times faced the problem, expressing his distress for the victims and their families, accepting responsibility, and pushing the government for more stringent safety regulations to prevent future outbreaks of this kind in the industry. McCain was also willing to pay the price through the recall costs and class action lawsuits. Maple Leaf Foods continues to thrive today and has the respect and loyalty of Canadian consumers.

The following is an excerpt from a press release in early 2009, only six months after the product recall:[8]

> *"While our profits were down 40% in the quarter, overshadowed by the product recall which, excluding one-time amounts, is estimated to have cost the Company $40 million to $50 million before taxes, there were many areas where we showed substantial improvement. Our packaged meats volumes have almost fully recovered, although we must demonstrate that consistently and we continue to experience significant margin compression. Overall we are pleased with the early progress made in recovering our packaged meats business, and are even more confident in the direction of our transformational efforts. We look forward to improving trends in 2009."*

Leadership and courage were required in order to face disaster and do the right thing to protect customers. They came directly from the top of the organization. By directly shouldering responsibility for this incident, Maple Leaf Foods created increased customer loyalty. They truly lived their stated values: "do what's right," "acting with integrity," and "treating people with respect."[9]

Wouldn't it be great if all organizations did this?

---

[7] As reported by the *Toronto Star*, April 14, 2009.

[8] Maple Leaf Press Release, February 24, 2009, "Maple Leaf Foods Reports Results for Fourth Quarter and Fiscal 2008. Recovery Progressing Well."

[9] From the Maple Leaf Foods website: http://www.mapleleaf.ca/Working/OurValues.aspx.

CHAPTER 15

What's Next?

So, how can you put the information in *The Customer Is Bothering Me* to work for you to get the results you need and solve the issues that come up? I recommend establishing a process to ensure that you stay focused on what is important. That way, you are much more likely to get the results you want and avoid the problem of starting something that does not get completed. Here's what I suggest:

1. **Set an outcome regarding what you want to achieve with your customers.** This could be a desired response rate for your direct marketing, volume or monetary value of sales over the next quarter, reduction in complaints received or escalations in a contact center, etc.

2. **Check out your organization's beliefs about customers.** The questions in Chapter 2 will help you figure out what drives the typical behaviors your people have with customers. **Review or create your Customer Philosophy,** with an eye to making sure you create a climate to foster the achievement of the outcomes you listed above. You can answer the questions listed in Chapter 5 either by yourself or as part of a team session. Team creation of the philosophy will get you more buy-in and commitment toward your outcomes.

3. **Identify the key procedures to use for sales, service, and problem transactions.** You can adapt these from the Words That Change Minds Customer Transaction Process and Upset Customer Process in Parts 3 and 4.

4. **Set up your Automatic Feedback Mechanisms to see how well you are doing at any given moment in time.** Make sure that it is easy for your customers to give you input and that they are thanked for doing so. Also implement your **Triggers of Change Mechanisms** so that the key people are ready to review, adapt, or change processes quickly and easily when you get sufficient evidence that something isn't working from your customers' point of view.

5. **Make sure everyone's roles and key behaviors are clear,** including conducting training sessions on new behavior expectations. When ev-

eryone on your team is briefed on what you expect and what you will measure, your success will be much easier. Have regular meetings to encourage and support your people. You can refer back to the Irish Continental Case Study in Chapter 13 for great tips.

6. **Repeat the above five steps regularly to ensure your outcomes and strategies will still be relevant** as the environment changes and new forces come into play.

Where else can you use the LAB Profile and the Words That Change Minds Customer Methodologies? You can question your happy customers to **understand more about the below-conscious aspects of their satisfaction** with you. If you knew the secrets to what makes them value your goods and services, you could also determine how to increase your customer base. Practice listening to LAB Profile Patterns as people speak to you—they are revealing what motivates them, usually without being aware of it.[1] Try out the Influencing Language and see for yourself how simple it can be to improve your relationships and find alternatives to conflicts. Don't wait until someone blows up to understand which Criteria and LAB Profile Patterns are driving them!

In Appendix D, there is a list of other ways you can benefit from knowing the LAB Profile, and in Appendix E, there is a description of the learning resources available to help you deepen your knowledge and ability to use these skills.

Bon voyage on your journey. Please let me know how the trip goes and what you discover along the way.

Shelle Rose Charvet
shelle@WordsThatChangeMinds.com

---

[1] For more practice, check out the *Understanding and Triggering Motivation, Increase Sales in Tough Times,* and *Solving Communication Programs with the LAB Profile* audio programs at www.TheShelle Store.com.

APPENDICES

APPENDIX A

Getting the Front Line to Make It Real

This appendix is designed to help team leaders and their teams bring the Customer Philosophy to life. When team leaders support their teams through practice and feedback, the front line is likely to use the processes and skills that you want them to be using. They are the ones who directly affect your customers' experience and gather critical information from customers to help you continually improve. To do this, they need to learn and practice the processes you want them to use.

Here you will find definitions of the techniques and skills as well as short exercises you can do with your team to have them practice.

Preparation for Team Leaders

Here are some questions and suggestions to help team leaders organize a training session for the front-line teams.

1. What is your organization's or team's Customer Philosophy? What do you believe about your customers and your offerings? How should this be apparent in the behavior of your sales and service staff? (See also Chapter 5.)
2. What is your step-by-step customer process for sales and service? How is it adapted for the different channels through which you communicate with your customers? (See also Chapter 6.)
3. In a meeting room away from the normal workspace, present an introduction of your Customer Philosophy, beliefs, and values to your team.
4. Plan for 15- to 45-minute training breaks twice per week to practice the skills and processes you've identified as necessary for superior sales and customer service. Have a bright, comfortable room for these training breaks and provide some healthy food to increase the pleasantness of the experience.

5. During each training break, have your team practice one part of the Normal Transaction Customer Process and then add in the subsequent parts so that they are able to go through each process with ease and handle difficult situations more easily.

Exercises for Team Meetings

Words That Change Minds Phone Tones© Round Robin

1. Write the names of the Phone Tones on separate slips of paper and distribute to team members. Ask players not to reveal which one they have.
2. One at a time, each team member says a few sentences in their given tone.
3. Other team members take turns guessing which tone is being used.
4. Team members exchange the tones after one round. This will help them identify which ones come naturally and which ones need more practice.

Rapport Role-Play

1. One team member role-plays as a phone-in client on a typical call.
2. The person playing the customer service representative listens and *matches* the speed of speech and inflection.
3. Observers give feedback on how well the customer service representative matched.
4. Switch roles so that everyone has a turn.

Rapport and Phone Tones

Advanced exercise:

1. One team member role-plays as a phone-in client on a typical call. You can use "dummy" phones or, if possible, live phones using the speakerphone function.
2. The person playing the customer service representative listens and matches the speed of speech and inflection. The rep uses the Special Event Tone while following the Greeting and Rapport step from the Words That Change Minds Customer Process.
3. Observers give feedback on tone and matching.
4. Switch roles so that everyone has a turn.

Funny Funnel Questions

1. One team member phones in as the client with several goofy requests, such as asking for a standard product with a list of changes to the product (similar to all those people you know who cannot order from the menu in a restaurant without a list of specific requests).
2. The customer service representative listens and tries to narrow down what is *really* important to the client by asking questions.
3. The representative can test by summarizing with the client's key words.
4. The customer service representative is done when the client agrees on what he/she wants.
5. Switch.

The Two-Solution Solution

1. A team member phones in as a client with a typical problem.
2. The customer service representative listens, summarizes what the client wants, and gets agreement.
3. The representative proposes two solutions using the Language of Suggestion and answers the Here's Why of each one.
4. The customer service representative helps the client make a decision and does a Double Check.
5. Observers check that the representative hit all these techniques, and the client reports back on how the experience felt.
6. Switch.

The Advanced Two-Solution Solution

1. A team member phones in as a client who is upset about a problem.
2. The customer service representative listens and summarizes what the client wants and gets agreement. The representative can also do Matching and Special Event and Curiosity Tones.
3. The representative proposes two solutions using the Language of Suggestion and answers the Here's Why of each one. The representative uses the Information Tone for credibility.
4. The customer service representative helps the client make a decision and does a Double Check.
5. Observers check that the representative hit all these techniques, and the client reports back on how the experience felt.
6. Switch.

Now and in the Future

1. Taking turns, each customer service representative practices three or four closing statements of their choice to Nourish the Relationship, using the Grateful Tone to say thank you and the Reassuring Tone to invite the customer to call any time they need something in order to *create a positive visual image of future experiences*.

   Hint: The language needs to be informal, rather than sounding like a script.

   Example:

   > "Any time you are at your desk creating the production reports and you have a question, you can just pick up the phone and we'll be right here to talk you through it."

2. Switch.

Leading and Giving Feedback on Exercises

Tips:

1. To improve someone's performance, make use of the Bad News Formula from Chapter 9. Give the bad news first in the form of a suggestion, then say "but" and give the good news last by saying what you liked.

   Example:

   > I suggest you speak a little slower to match this client's speed, but you did a great Special Event Tone, and you sounded very comfortable and inviting.

2. For more detailed improvement instructions, use the Suggestion Model:
   a. Make the suggestion.
   b. Explain here's why:
      1. what it would accomplish (Toward Language), and
      2. what it would prevent or avoid (Away From Language).
   c. End with overall encouraging statement.

   Example:

   > I was thinking you might try switching from the Special Event Tone to the Information Tone when you were proposing the two solutions. This would let the customer know that you had important information to give them and avoid them doubting what you are saying. This should be pretty easy for you because you are good at switching tones.

3. Ensure the sales and service staff are speaking informally—this is the opposite of sounding like they are following a script. They can be informal and still sound very professional.
4. Laugh a lot with the group during the exercises, creating positive associations with the techniques.

Encourage each sales or service staff member to do their own feedback and ask what they learned from the experience.

Summary of Key Techniques and Processes

TABLE A-1 — **Words That Change Minds Customer Transaction Process**

1. Greeting and Rapport	2. Needs Determination	3. Knowledge and Solutions	4. Nourish the Relationship
Special Event Tone	**Funnel Questions**	Explain next steps: **Procedure Language** with **Information Tone**	Check if there is anything else
Rapport: Match client's inflection, speed of speech, and key words	**Curiosity Tone** **Summarize** what client wants	Get **Permission** to make suggestions	Say thanks with **Grateful Tone**
	Repeat Client's Key Words	When appropriate, offer **Two Solutions** to give client choice	"Anyone here would be delighted to help," use **Reassuring Tone**
	Get agreement ("Is that right?")	Use the **Language of Suggestion** and the **Here's Why Approach**	Create a **visual image** in the client's mind of **future positive experiences**
		Ask which solution client prefers	
		Double-Check to verify client is okay with solution using **Client's Key Words**	

TABLE A-2   **Customer Tone Chart©**

Customer Tone	Your Response	Desired Response from Customer
Neutral	Warm, friendly	Warm tone of voice
Concerned, worried	Surprised, concerned, committed to finding a solution	Relieved
Annoyed, irritated	Surprised, concerned, committed to finding a solution	Calmer
Panic	Shock, horror, and dismay, committed to finding a solution	Calmer
Furious	Shock, horror, and dismay, committed to finding a solution	Calmer

TABLE A-3   **Words That Change Minds Phone Tones©**

Name of Tone	Purpose	Description	Desired Response
Special Event Tone	To let the client know this conversation is special to you too	Quiet enthusiasm	Client becomes more enthusiastic
Curiosity Tone	To show you are interested	Tone up on the end of sentences	Client gives you the information you need
Information Tone	To provide information in a credible way	Keep tone even, credible, monotone, down at end of sentences	Client believes what you say
Grateful Tone	To show appreciation for the client's patronage	Warm tone, emphasis on "you" in "thank you"	Client becomes warm and friendly
Reassuring Tone	To set up a positive experience for the next time the client needs to call	Comforting, friendly	Client expresses appreciation

Words That Change Minds Customer Communication Techniques

1. **Rapport**: Match client's tone, inflection, and speed of speech to get on the same wavelength with the client from the first few words.
2. **Funnel Questions:** Start with open-ended questions and gradually narrow down to the essential.
3. **Client's Key Words:** Pay attention to words and phrases the customer stresses or repeats. These indicate importance in the client's mind. Try using them as you reply.

4. **Procedure Language:** Use "First step," "Second step," and "Last step," as well as "Here's how," so the customer knows that you know what to do.

5. **Two-Solution Solution:** Offer two options so the client gains a sense of control as they get to make the final decision while you are giving them guidance.

6. **Language of Suggestion:** Propose and offer rather than tell.

7. **Double-Check:** Repeat a decision to give the client the chance to express any doubts or reaffirm the choice, using the client's key words.

8. **Permission:** Ask if it's all right before moving on; this ensures agreement.

9. **Here's Why Approach:** Explain the benefits and problems solved by taking each of the solutions.

10. **Nourish the Relationship:** Create a visual image in the client's mind of future positive experiences with your organization. Invite the client to call again any time they need something in order to set up a positive experience for future calls. Reassure the customer that they will be well cared for the next time.

TABLE A-4 ——————————————**Words That Change Minds Upset Customer Process**

1. Treat the Emotion First	2. Clarify What the Customer Wants and Take Action	3. Make Amends	4. Nourish the Relationship
1. Be upset on behalf of your customer.	Offer Two Options	Make Amends Policy	Set up a positive expectation for the future
2. Match their tone.	Use Language of Suggestion and Language of Prevention	"I" Language	
3. Say something helpful.		Special Event Tone	Reassuring Tone
4. Lead the tone to a lower level.			Create a visual image in the client's mind of future positive experiences

TABLE A-5 ——————— **Upset Customer LAB Profile Patterns**

Normal Interaction	Upset Customer LAB Profile Patterns	Language of Influence to Use	Words to Avoid	Desired Response
External (willing to follow instructions)	**Internal** (won't be told what to do)	**The Language of Suggestion,** e.g., I suggest, Here's what we could do	**Directive Language,** e.g., Do this, Go here, Speak to Mr. Vargas	Considering, then accepting
Toward a goal or **Away From** a problem	Highly **Away From** the present problem	**The Language of Prevention:** "I want to make sure that it won't happen again."	**Giving instructions** to customer without a reason	Cooperation
Procedures (will follow normal process)	**Options** (wants you to break rules to fix this!)	**The Special Way:** Usually I have to . . . but because of this problem, I'm going to . . .	**The Normal Procedure**	Renewed cooperation
Mainly Thing (focused on the TASK)	**Person** (wants YOU to help)	**The Personal Touch:** "I can help you, Mr. Lee"	**Thing Language:** It will have to go for repair	A personal relationship
Neutral Emotions	**High Feelings** (very negative emotional state)	**Match upset tone** of customer (see Customer Tone Chart©)	Sounding as if the problem is a **normal occurrence**	Customer calms down

All exercises and principles can be adapted to the kind of communication and/or situation in which you work with your customers, whether by phone, in person, etc. They are also a way to identify areas of improvement and strengths in your customer service team, and may provide you with ideas for where your system needs improvement.

When you set up a special place and create a fun atmosphere where your team can learn together, your people are more likely to integrate the messages you want and to guide your customers through a caring experience. This is a great way to live the experience you want your customers to have.

Every leader sets the tone for their team, and what you create gets passed down and through your team. If you set the example, as the leaders in the Region of Halton, the Irish Continental Ferries Group, and the Maple Leaf Foods Group did, your staff will follow your example and do their best to intelligently take care of your present and future customers in each contact.

LAB Profile Customer Questionnaire

			Motivation Triggers
Questions	*Category*	*Patterns*	*Indicators*
(no question – just listen)	**Level**	**Proactive** **Reactive**	—action verbs, do it, now —thinking, waiting, passive verbs
What do you want? What is important to you about . . . ?	**Criteria**		(note exact words used)
Why is that important?	**Direction of Movement**	**Toward** **Away From**	—gain, attain, positive benefits, achieve —don't want, avoid, prevent, solve
How would you know that you had done a good job at . . . ?	**Source**	**Internal** **External**	—decides for self, I know, my standards —influenced by others, outside evidence
Why did you choose your last . . .?	**Reason**	**Options** **Procedures**	—list of reasons, why, alternatives, choice —story, facts, how it happened
What is the relationship between this one and the last one you purchased?	**Decision Factors**	**Sameness** **Sameness with Exception** **Difference**	—same, as always, the usual —improve, upgrade, same but, progressing —different, new, changed, switch, shift

Working Traits

Questions	Category	Patterns	Indicators
(no question – just listen)	**Scope**	**Specific**	—details, lots of information
		General	—overview, main points, big picture
Tell me about a situation when this kind of buying decision was a problem.	**Stress Response**	**Feelings**	—gets and stays emotional
		Choice	—gets emotional and comes out
		Thinking	—doesn't become emotional
Tell me about a situation when what you bought was (their Criteria).	**Style**	**Independent**	—alone, I, sole responsibility
		Proximity	—says I but others involved
		Cooperative	—we, team, shared responsibility
What did you like about that?	**Organization**	**Person**	—people, feelings, relationships
		Thing	—things, systems, results, tasks
How would you know if someone else bought a great . . . ?	**Convincer Channel**	**See**	—see, watch, look at
		Hear	—hear, discuss, conversation
		Read	—read, reports, documents
		Do	—do, try it out, try it on
How many times would you have to (insert answer from previous page) to be *convinced* they bought a great . . . ?	**Convincer Mode**	**Number of Examples**	—needs a certain number of times
		Automatic	—knows right away, instantly
		Consistent	—not completely convinced
		Period of Time	—needs a duration

Note: For the purposes of interacting with customers, I have eliminated the Attention Direction and Rule Structure Categories from the above questionnaire, as they are most likely not relevant.

APPENDIX C

Influencing Language Shortcuts

Phrases to use for influencing and persuading.

MOTIVATION TRAITS

LEVEL

Proactive—do it, go for it, jump in, now, get it done, don't wait

Reactive—understand, think about, wait, analyze, consider, wait, might, could, would

DIRECTION

Toward—attain, obtain, have, get, include, achieve

Away From—avoid, steer clear of, get rid of, exclude, solve, fix

SOURCE

External—so and so thinks, the feedback you'll get, the approval you'll get, others will notice, give references

Internal—only you can decide, you know it's up to you, what do you think

REASON

Options—break the rules just for them, opportunity, choice, expanding, options, alternatives, possibilities

Procedures—speak in procedures: first . . . then . . . after which; the right way, tried and true, tell them about the procedures they will get to use

DECISION FACTORS

Sameness—same as, in common, as you always do, like before, unchanged, as you know

Sameness with Exception—more, better, less, same except, evolving, progress, gradual improvement

Difference—new, totally different, completely changed, switch, shift, unique, revolutionary, brand new

Sameness with Exception and Difference—(both Sameness with Exception and Difference vocabulary will work)

WORKING TRAITS
SCOPE

Specific—exactly, precisely, specifically (and give lots of details in sequence)

General—the big picture, essentially, the important thing is, in general, concepts

ATTENTION DIRECTION

Self—keep communication focused on the content

Other—influenced by the depth of rapport

STYLE

Independent—do it alone, by yourself, you alone, without interruption, total control

Proximity—you'll be in charge, around others, you'll direct, your responsibility is X, theirs is Y

Cooperative—us, we, together, all of us, team, group, share responsibility, do it together, let's

ORGANIZATION

Person—use personal pronouns and people's names, feelings, thoughts, feel good, people

Thing—impersonal pronouns: things, systems, process, task, job, goal, organization

STRESS RESPONSE

Feelings—empathy, happy, intense, exciting, mind boggling, wonderful

Choice—empathy, appropriate, makes good sense and feels right

Thinking—clear thinking, logical, rational, cold reality, hard facts, statistics

RULE STRUCTURE

My/My—you know what you want and what they need, when it's clear to you, what goes for the goose goes for the gander

My/.—doing what you want, when you want, whatever the price

No/My—even if you aren't sure, when you don't know what to do next

My/Your—different strokes for different folks, everyone is not the same

CONVINCER CHANNEL

See—must see data to get convinced

Hear—must hear data to get convinced

Read—must read data to get convinced

Do—must do it to get convinced

CONVINCER MODE

Number of Examples—use the person's number

Automatic—assume, benefit of the doubt

Consistent—try it, each time you use it, daily, every time, consistent

Period of Time—match period of time

Other LAB Profile Practical Applications

The following are some of the applications graduates of the LAB Profile Consultant/Trainer Certification Program have been creating over the years.

- **Marketing Research:** Since these patterns vary by context, several methodologies have been developed to empirically determine the different below-conscious motivations customers have for competing products and services. This is used to create whole mass communication strategies.

- **Coaching:** I developed a methodology using the LAB Profile called Conversational Coaching, whereby the coach elicits conversationally the LAB Profile Patterns of the present and desired state and casually overlaps the Influencing Language to enable the client to experience the desired state and develop his or her own solutions.

- **Training for Behavior Change:** Using the LAB Profile, you can choose activities that will create the desired behavior changes for any target group, first by decoding the Motivation Patterns for the group and then by understanding which LAB Profile Patterns are addressed by any given activity.

- **People Management:** You can train managers to identify the LAB Profile Patterns and thereby the strengths of their team members, so they can adjust assignments to suit what staff members naturally do best at work.

- **Recruitment:** You can do a LAB Profile for a position and corporate culture to create an advertisement that will be irresistible to those who fit and turn off those who do not fit. You can screen the selected short-listed candidates to find the best match. (*Note:* The LAB Profile does not measure skills, knowledge, or attitude; rather, it measures whether the person has the Motivation Traits and Internal Processing to fit the tasks and the environment. In other words, it assesses "fit.")

- **Skills Training:** Learning the LAB Profile will enable people to develop finely tuned abilities in the following areas: influencing and persuading, negotiating, leadership, conflict resolution, sales, and customer service.

- **Consulting and Problem-Solving:** I developed an easy-to-use LAB Profile methodology to diagnose and develop solutions to any communication problem. This is a favorite among business leaders and consultants.

- **Implementing Organizational Change:** You can diagnose the present and desired organizational cultures in LAB Profile terms and determine the appropriate change methodology for maximum sustainable results.

- **Team Building:** When you do a team LAB Profile, you can determine the team's strengths and weaknesses with regards to their mandate. You can also identify communication patterns within the team and between the team and others, as well as determine the Patterns of the next person needed for the team.

- **Teaching and Learning:** Teachers and students can easily identify the LAB Profile Patterns that facilitate or cause difficulties in learning for individuals and whole groups. Minor adjustments can then be made to the teaching/learning methodology to correct any problems. I gave a workshop to the National Indian Education Conference in Canada (for teachers on Native Indian reservations) on how to prevent dropouts by using this methodology.

- **Modeling:** The LAB Profile Patterns can be used to decode any strategy or skill, simply by identifying the behaviors (internal and external) used. You can conduct a LAB Profile to determine which Patterns are at play when an exemplar demonstrates their skill.

LAB Profile Learning Resources

Words That Change Minds: Mastering the Language of Influence

Book by Shelle Rose Charvet

Words That Change Minds is the international LAB Profile bestseller that will give you new ways of thinking about individuals and groups to help you get what you want! You will learn how to notice how people unconsciously get motivated, process information, and make decisions; use Irresistible Influencing Language; decode any communication problem and solve it; pry open mental space in even the most closed of minds; and establish rapport and credibility with anyone!

There are applications for sales, marketing, hiring, negotiation, teaching, training, and improving any relationship.

Understanding & Triggering Motivation: The LAB Profile

6 CD/MP3 Series
Companion to *Words That Change Minds*
Shelle Rose Charvet

No time to read *Words That Change Minds*? Do you spend a lot of time in your car? Learn how to motivate and influence people by listening in your car or on the train. This program, recorded live with a group and professionally edited, contains great information and lively demonstrations.

Do you have to deal with negative or difficult people? Learn the Influencing Language to open the doors.

Conversational Coaching with the LAB Profile

1-hour CD/MP3 with Reference Guide
Advanced LAB Profile Series
Shelle Rose Charvet

Help others help themselves, by listening to how they speak.

In this program, Shelle shows you how to apply the LAB Profile Patterns in informal coaching conversations to decode your client's problem, identify the key patterns of the solution, and use the right words to help the client shift naturally into solution mode.

Since much of coaching really happens outside of the official coaching session—for example, in the hallway, on a phone call, or as a "by the way"—this CD gives you just the right informal approach.

Shelle introduces Conversational Coaching©, an informal, yet highly effective coaching methodology now used by certified coaches around the world.

This program includes:

- A live demonstration of the Conversational Coaching© process
- A detailed debriefing to identify what to listen for
- How to decode the client's problem and their solution via LAB Profile Patterns
- Testing your diagnosis for accuracy using rigorous empirical and scientific methodology
- Influencing Language to shift the client into their own solution mode
- Verbal and nonverbal ways to get permission to help
- How to ensure your client will succeed

If you are familiar with the LAB Profile and want to use it in coaching conversations, this program will show you how. Includes CD and reference guide.

Solving Communication Problems with the LAB Profile

1-hour CD/MP3
Advanced LAB Profile Series
Shelle Rose Charvet

This program shows you how to uncover what is motivating people in a conflict, how to create innovative communication strategies to solve intractable problems, and how to find the leverage point that makes the difference. Discover the key people to influence—even when they are not present. Use the right language to persuade anyone.

You will learn how to use the LAB Profile to decode any communication challenge and create solutions that work using just the right language.

Learn a four-step LAB Profile Process to solve your most difficult communication challenges.

This program includes:

- How to identify what is driving people by decoding their behavior
- Creating innovative communication strategies to solve intractable problems
- Finding the leverage point that makes the difference
- Uncovering the key people to influence—even when they are not present
- How to find the right language to persuade anyone
- Two demonstrations with a Q & A that makes the process easy to learn

Create a bigger impact and have more influence at work and at home.

Presenting Ideas to Skeptical People

1-hour CD/MP3
Shelle Rose Charvet

Have you ever had a great idea shot down by a skeptic?

Why do you have to spend so much mental energy dealing with negative people?

What if you could identify and resolve doubts, reservations, hesitations, and objections and get people to really listen?

This program covers how to deal with the "macho" person who already knows everything. Learn why many people fail to be convincing. Experience a four-step process for getting even the most conscientious of objectors to take your ideas seriously.

Shelle demonstrates the Skeptical People Process; the three points of view crucial to being convincing; how to use common experiences to get your point across; how to pry open mental space in even the most closed of minds; and how to make sure your message passes "The Macho Test."

Building Long-Term Relationships with Clients: Decode What Your Customer Really Wants

1-hour CD/MP3
Shelle Rose Charvet

Have you ever wanted to get inside your customer's head and heart? Wouldn't it be great if you could find out what they never tell you directly?

If your business success depends on your ability to predict and fulfill your clients' unstated psychological needs, this program will show you how to:

- Find out what really motivates your customers
- Read between the lines to keep your customers happy

- Use your surveys to go beyond the obvious
- Make sure you use the right Influencing Language to match what your customers want to hear
- Avoid turning the customer off

Plus there is a special sheet included with examples of client feedback, decoded for you!

Only Pick a Fight When You Can Win! How to Turn a Confrontation into a Conversation

1-hour CD/MP3
Shelle Rose Charvet

What to do if someone just won't agree? And what if you are uncomfortable confronting or saying no?

This program covers how to manage your emotions, how to find out what is important to you and the other person, how to solve differences, and how to reach a solution that you both want. Learn the steps to solving conflicts with other people, both at work and at home.

Shelle demonstrates how to know when *not* to pick a fight; how to identify an issue worth solving; getting ready to tackle a conflict; creating common goals worth pursuing; elegantly overcoming resistance and non-cooperation; calming negative emotions immediately; getting what you need; and avoiding the Two Extremes Trap!

Articles on Influencing and Persuasion

To receive Shelle's new ideas and applications and upcoming events, subscribe to Shelle's Irregular E-Newsletter on influencing and persuasion at www.WordsThatChangeMinds.com.

It is Shelle's firm commitment that this newsletter will come out at no particular time.

Shelle's Blog: www.TheShelleBlog.com
Shelle's Articles: www.ShellesArticles.com
Shelle's Videos: www.ShellesVideos.com
Shelle's Learning Products: www.TheShelleStore.com

Mobile LAB Profile Resources

Do you want a quick shortcut to the LAB Profile Questions for Sales, the Influencing Language, or the Macho Test? Check out my mobile resource site directly from your Blackberry, iPhone, or mobile phone:

www.LABProfile.mobi

You can bookmark this site and refer to it any time.

Here's what it will look like on your handheld device:

WELCOME TO THE WORDS THAT CHANGE MINDS LAB PROFILE MOBILE RESOURCE CENTER

Frequent Requests

LAB Profile Questions for Sales
LAB Profile Pattern Summaries
Influencing Language Short Cut
Hints for Dealing with Macho Types
LAB Profile Questions for HR and Managers

Click here to email Shelle directly to ask questions, make a suggestion or to let us know if this site has been helpful.

Click here to go to our main site.

APPENDIX F

Conferences, Keynotes, and Learning Programs

If you are looking for a dynamic speaker to energize your people and give them new insights and skills, check me out!

Do you need someone to inspire and inform your people, and work with groups to solve their influencing and persuasion challenges?

To book Shelle Rose Charvet (in English or French) to address your conference or event, or to have me design a learning program in influencing and persuasion for you, please contact:

Success Strategies/Stratégies de réussite
1 866 442 6468 toll free from the USA and Canada
+ 1 (905) 639-6468

www.WordsThatChangeMinds.com

LAB Profile Training Opportunities

For LAB Profile training in your area, **consult the list of certified international trainers and consultants** at www.WordsThatChangeMinds.com in the Tools and Resources section.

Check out Shelle's international events at www.ShellesEvents.com.

For information on the **LAB Profile Consultant/Trainer Certification Program** and the **LAB Profile Advanced Business Applications Certificate**, please visit www.LABProfileCertification.com.

Your feedback is welcome about any of the ideas expressed in this book.

Please contact me directly:

shelle@WordsThatChangeMinds.com
1 866 442 6468 toll free from the USA and Canada
+ 1 (905) 639-6468

Shelle Rose Charvet

INDEX